EXTREME
PUZZLES
FROM
THE
BIBLE

**INCLUDING CROSSWORDS,
WORD SEARCH, CRYPTOGRAMS, AND MORE**

TIMOTHY E. PARKER

HOWARD BOOKS
A DIVISION OF SIMON & SCHUSTER, INC.

New York · Nashville · London · Toronto · Sydney · New Delhi

Howard Books
A Division of Simon & Schuster, Inc.
1230 Avenue of the Americas
New York, NY 10020

First Howard Books trade paperback edition October 2011

HOWARD and colophon are trademarks of Simon & Schuster, Inc.

For information about special discounts for bulk purchases, please contact Simon & Schuster Special Sales at 1-866-506-1949 or business@simonandschuster.com.

The Simon & Schuster Speakers Bureau can bring authors to your live event. For more information or to book an event, contact the Simon & Schuster Speakers Bureau at 1-866-248-3049 or visit our website at www.simonspeakers.com.

Manufactured in the United States of America

10 9 8 7 6 5 4 3 2 1

ISBN 978-1-4391-9230-6

Part One
CRYPTOGRAMS

Bible Cryptograms Introduction: How to Play

Cryptograms are an extremely fun way to learn and solve Scriptures. You will have to decipher the coded letters of each puzzle, but I leave a HUGE hint for each one. To solve a cryptogram, you must substitute the coded letter for the real letter it represents in a Bible verse. For example, in the sample on the following page, if you figure out that the first letter of the puzzle, in this case a V, is actually an A, then you may substitute each and every V in the coded puzzle with an A. If you determine the next letter in the puzzle, in this case an F, is actually an N, then simply substitute all Fs in the puzzle with Ns. Simply write your new letters on the blank lines directly under the coded letters.

How Do I Know What the Coded Letters Really Are?

Here's that huge hint I promised: See the title of the puzzle in parentheses, "WHO SEEK YOU."? That is an ACTUAL section of the real answer. You may count the letters and match it up to the coded letters, and you've just been given several of the coded letters! Did you notice the period in the title (WHO SEEK YOU.)? That's a big hint that the words given are at the end of the sentence.

In the sample below, the bold letters in the coded puzzle show you where the title words (WHO SEEK YOU) are. Now you know that the letter M is actually the letter W and the letter R is actually the letter H and so on.

One final hint: The last part of every puzzle is the Bible book with verse and chapter. If you can find out which book is mentioned, you will be given extra letters to solve the puzzle.

And one last, finally final hint: Single letters in the coded puzzle will probably be an A or I. Make sense?

SAMPLE: (WHO SEEK YOU.)

VFO ARBLK MRB XFBM PBWE FVDK ZWA ARKIE

___ _____ ___ _____ ____

____ ___ _____

AEWLA IF PBW,

_____ __ ___,

SBE PBW, B GBEO, RVNK FBA SBELVXKF ARBLK

___ ____

MRB LKKX PBW.

<u>W</u> H O <u>S</u> E E <u>K</u> <u>Y</u> O <u>U</u>.

ZLVGD 9:10

_ _ _ _ _ 9:10

SOLUTION

And those who know your name put their trust in you,
for you, O Lord, have not forsaken those who seek you.
Psalm 9:10

PUZZLE 1: (THAT DAY ABOUT THREE)

EB GWBEC QWB HCLCAXCM WAE QBHM QCHC

__ _____ ___ _____

___ ____ ____

NJOGAPCM, JTM GWCHC QCHC JMMCM GWJG

_____, ___ _____ ____

_____ ____

MJI JNBSG GWHCC GWBSEJTM EBSZE.

___ _____ _____

_____ _____.

JLGE 2:41

_ _ _ _ 2:41

PUZZLE 2: (AND INDIVIDUALLY)

QI UC, ZSIHVS LGXO, GWC IXC AIBO JX MSWJQZ,

__ __, _____ ____, ___

___ ____ __ _____,

GXB JXBJFJBHGNNO LCLACWQ IXC IE GXIZSCW.

___ _____

_____ ___ __ _____.

WILGXQ 12:5

_ _ _ _ _ _ 12:5

PUZZLE 3: (NOT DISMAYED, FOR)

RQTD GVJ, RVD Z TP LZJY EVA;

____ ___—, ___ _ __ ____
___;

CQ GVJ XZUPTEQX, RVD Z TP EVAD HVX;

__ ___ _____—, ___ _ __
____ ___;

Z LZKK UJDQGHJYQG EVA, Z LZKK YQKO EVA,

_ ____ _____ ___, _
____ ____ ___,

Z LZKK AOYVKX EVA LZJY PE DZHYJQVAU DZHYJ

_ ____ _____ ___ ____
__ _____ _____

YTGX.

____.

ZUTZTY 41:10

__,_____ 41:10

PUZZLE 4: (THEY HAD BEEN WITH)

XCT TNHX DNHR EMT DNH SCIVXHEE CJ FHDHP

___ ____ ____ ___ ___

_____ __ _____

MXV QCNX, MXV FHPYHBWHV DNMD DNHR
THPH

___ ____, ___ _____

____ ____ ____

KXHVKYMDHV, YCOOCX OHX, DNHR THPH

_____, _____ ___,

____ ____

MEDCXBENHV. MXV DNHR PHYCZXBGHV DNMD

_____. ___ ____

_____ ____

DNHR NMV SHHX TBDN QHEKE.

____ ___ ____ ____ _____.

MYDE 4:13

_ _ _ _ 4:13

PUZZLE 5: (SET MY FACE LIKE)

MOZ ZTD WBIK NBK TDWXL FD;

___ ___ ____ ___ _____

_ _;

ZTDIDCBID J TPYD GBZ MDDG KJLNIPHDK;

_____ _ _____ ___

____ _____;

ZTDIDCBID J TPYD LDZ FE CPHD WJVD P CWJGZ,

_____ _ ____ ___ __

____ ____ _ _____,

PGK J VGBQ ZTPZ J LTPWW GBZ MD XOZ ZB

___ _ ____ ____ _ _____

___ __ ___ __

LTPFD.

_____.

JLPJPT 50:7

_ _____ 50:7

PUZZLE 6: (ONE ANOTHER TO LOVE)

LYI SFM WJ QUYJHIFG NUC MU JMHG WO UYF

___ ___ __ _____ ___

__ ____ __ ___

LYUMNFG MU SUAF LYI TUUI CUGVJ, YUM

_____ __ ____ ___ ____

_____, ___

YFTSFQMHYT MU RFFM MUTFMNFG, LJ HJ MNF

_____ __ ____

_____, __ __ ___

NLEHM UB JURF, EWM FYQUWGLTHYT UYF

_____ __ ____, ___

_____ ___

LYUMNFG, LYI LSS MNF RUGF LJ XUW JFF MNF

_____, ___ ___ ___ ____

__ ___ ___ ___

ILX IGLCHYT YFLG.

___ _____ ____.

NFEGFCJ 10:24–25

_____ 10:24–25

PUZZLE 7: (WHY HE IS NOT ASHAMED)

VNF MC UMN TLIKWEVECT LIX WMNTC UMN
LFC

___ __ ___ _____
___ _____ ___ ___

TLIKWEVECX LBB MLZC NIC TNAFKC. WMLW ET

_____ ___ ____ ___
_____. ____ __

UMR MC ET INW LTMLOCX WN KLBB WMCO

___ __ __ ___ _____ __
____ ____

JFNWMCFT, TLREIS,

_____, _____,

"E UEBB WCBB NV RNAF ILOC WN OR JFNWMCFT;

"_ ____ ____ __ ____ ____
__ __ _____;

EI WMC OEXTW NV WMC KNISFCSLWENI E UEBB

__ ___ _____ __ ___
_____ _ ____

TEIS RNAFYFLETC."

____ ____ _____."

MCJFCUT 2:11–12

_____ 2:11–12

PUZZLE 8: (YOU. AND I BELIEVE IT)

ZED LB DGF SYUUYJLBC LBHDIEVDLYBH L MY

___ __ ___ _____

_____ _ __

BYD VYXXFBM AYE, ZFVREHF JGFB AYE VYXF

___ _____ ___, _____

____ ___ ____

DYCFDGFI LD LH BYD SYI DGF ZFDDFI ZED SYI

_____ __ __ ___ ___

___ _____ ___ ___

DGF JYIHF. SYI, LB DGF SLIHD OURVF, JGFB AYE

___ _____. ___, __ ___

_____ _____, ____ ___

VYXF DYCFDGFI RH R VGEIVG, L GFRI DGRD

____ _____ __ _

_____, _ ____ ____

DGFIF RIF MLQLHLYBH RXYBC AYE. RBM L

_____ ___ _____

_____ ___. ___ _

ZFULFQF LD LB ORID,

_____ __ __ ____,

1 VYILBDGLRBH 11:17–18

1 _ _ _ _ _ _ _ _ _ _ _ _ 11:17–18

PUZZLE 9: (OF GOD, FOR APART)

FGDMD SA VWFGSVRYDFFDM BWM H JDMAWV

_ _ _ _ _   _ _   _ _ _ _ _ _ _ _   _ _ _ _ _ _

_ _ _   _   _ _ _ _ _ _

FGHV FGHF GD AGWLNC DHF HVC CMSVZ HVC

_ _ _ _   _ _ _ _   _ _   _ _ _ _ _ _   _ _ _

_ _ _   _ _ _ _ _   _ _ _

BSVC DVOWKUDVF SV GSA FWSN. FGSA HNAW, S

_ _ _ _   _ _ _ _ _ _ _ _ _ _   _ _   _ _ _

_ _ _ _.   _ _ _ _   _ _ _ _,   _

AHI, SA BMWU FGD GHVC WB RWC, BWM HJHMF

_ _ _,   _ _   _ _ _ _   _ _ _   _ _ _ _   _ _

_ _ _,   _ _ _   _ _ _ _ _

BMWU GSU IGW THV DHF WM IGW THV GHXD

_ _ _ _   _ _ _   _ _ _   _ _ _   _ _ _   _ _

_ _ _   _ _ _   _ _ _ _

DVOWKUDVF?

_ _ _ _ _ _ _ _ _?

DTTNDASHAFDA 2:24–25

_ _ _ _ _ _ _ _ _ _ _ _ _ 2:24–25

PUZZLE 10: (NOT BE AFRAID OF)

RT JTL PU XGIXOR TG NWRRUJ LUIITI

__ ___ __ _____ __

_____ _____

TI TG LKU IWOJ TG LKU EOBAUR, EKUJ OL
BTVUN,

__ __ ___ ____ __ ___

_____, ____ __ _____,

GTI LKU QTIR EOQQ PU STWI BTJGORUJBU

___ ___ ____ ____ __

____ _____

XJR EOQQ AUUF STWI GTTL GITV PUOJH

___ ____ ____ ____ ____

____ _____

BXWHKL.

_____.

FITDUIPN 3:25–26

_____ 3:25–26

PUZZLE 11: (FOOD, AND ONE OF)

WE B NPJSYMP JP IWISMP WI HJJPKQ TKJSYMZ

__ _ _____ __ _____

__ _____ _____

BLZ KBTOWLV WL ZBWKQ EJJZ, BLZ JLM JE QJF

___ _____ __ _____

_____, ___ ___ __ ___

IBQI SJ SYMA, "VJ WL HMBTM, NM GBPAMZ BLZ

____ __ _____, "__ __ _____,

__ _____ ___

EWKKMZ," GWSYJFS VWDWLV SYMA SYM

_____," _____ _____

____ ___

SYWLVI LMMZMZ EJP SYM NJZQ, GYBS VJJZ WI

_____ _____ ___ ___

____, ____ ____ __

SYBS?

____?

XBAMI 2:15–16

_____ 2:15–16

PUZZLE 12: (HONOR THE LORD WITH)

NXHXF DNY UXFC TSDN LXAF TYKUDN

_____ ___ ____ ____ ____

_____

KHC TSDN DNY RSFGDRFASDG XR KUU LXAF

___ ____ ___

_____ __ ___ ____

OFXCAQY;

_____;

DNYH LXAF ZKFHG TSUU ZY RSUUYC TSDN

____ ____ _____ ____ __

_____ ____

OUYHDL,

_____,

KHC LXAF EKDG TSUU ZY ZAFGDSHM TSDN
TSHY.

___ ____ ____ ____ __

_____ ____ ____.

OFXEYFZG 3:9–10

_____ 3:9–10

PUZZLE 13: (OF THE DILIGENT)

MOA DCWV VCAR KCM DAM MOA WPZOMACHR

___ ____ ____ ___ ___

___ _____

ZC OHKZWB,

__ _____,

EHM OA MOLGWMR MOA NWGYPKZ CU MOA

___ __ _____ ___

_____ __ ___

LPNXAV.

_____.

G RDGNX OGKV NGHRAR QCYAWMB,

_ _____ ____ _____

_____,

EHM MOA OGKV CU MOA VPDPZAKM TGXAR

___ ___ ____ __ ___

_____ _____

WPNO.

____.

QWCYAWER 10:3–4

_____ 10:3–4

PUZZLE 14: (TO DIE IS GAIN.)

SHJ ZH PQ ZH UFAQ FR XVJFRZ, GMK ZH KFQ FR

___ __ __ __ ____ __

_____, ___ __ ___ __

CGFM. FS F GP ZH UFAQ FM ZVQ SUQRV, ZVGZ

____. __ _ __ __ ____ __

___ _____, ____

PQGMR SJTFZSTU UGEHJ SHJ PQ. NQZ LVFXV F

_____ _____ _____

___ __. ___ _____ _

RVGUU XVHHRQ F XGMMHZ ZQUU. F GP VGJK

_____ _____ _ _____

____. _ __ ____

BJQRRQK EQZLQQM ZVQ ZLH. PN KQRFJQ FR ZH

_____ _____ ___ ___.

__ _____ __ ___

KQBGJZ GMK EQ LFZV XVJFRZ, SHJ ZVGZ FR SGJ

_____ ___ __ ____

_____, ___ ____ __ ___

EQZZQJ. ETZ ZH JQPGFM FM ZVQ SUQRV FR

_____. ___ __ _____ __

___ _____ __

PHJQ MQXQRRGJN HM NHTJ GXXHTMZ.

____ _____ __ ____
_____.

BVFUFBBFGMR 1:21–24

_____ 1:21–24

PUZZLE 15: (HIM WENT OUT THROUGH ALL)

GYK WATVT FALVFYAK XY LZA INMAF NH LZA

___ _____ _____ __
___ _____ __ ___

TIXFXL LN PGUXUAA, GYK G FAINFL GQNVL ZXD

_____ __ _____, ___ _
_____ _____ ___

MAYL NVL LZFNVPZ GUU LZA TVFFNVYKXYP

____ ___ _____ ___ ___
_____

ONVYLFC. GYK ZA LGVPZL XY LZAXF

_____. ___ __ _____ __
_____

TCYGPNPVAT, QAXYP PUNFXHXAK QC GUU.

_____, _____
_____ __ ___.

GYK ZA OGDA LNYGEGFALZ, MZAFA ZA ZGK

___ __ ____ __ _____,
_____ __ ___

QAAY QFNVPZL VI. GYK GT MGT ZXT OVTLND, ZA

____ _____ __. ___ __

___ ___ _____, __

MAYL LN LZA TCYGPNPVA NY LZA TGQQGLZ

____ __ ___ _____ __

___ _____

KGC, GYK ZA TLNNK VI LN FAGK.

___, ___ __ _____ __ __

____.

UVSA 4:14–16

____ 4:14–16

> How can anyone lose who chooses to become a Christian?
> If, when he dies, there turns out to be no God and his faith was
> vain, he has lost nothing — in fact, he has been happier in life than his
> non-believing friends. If, however, there is a God and a heaven and
> hell, then he has gained heaven, and his skeptical friends will have lost
> everything in hell.
> —Francis Bacon, English philosopher, scientist, and lawyer. He served
> as both attorney general and lord chancellor of England and
> was responsible for popularizing an inductive methodology
> for scientific inquiry known as the scientific method.

PUZZLE 16: (WE SEE HIM WHO)

JDI EL ZLL FPH EFT UTY N RPIIRL EFPRL ENZ

___ __ ___ ___ ___ ___ _

_____ _____ ___

HNML RTELY IFNV IFL NVXLRZ, VNHLRK GLZDZ,

____ _____ ____ ___

_____, _____ _____,

BYTEVLM EPIF XRTYK NVM FTVTY JLBNDZL TU

_____ ____ _____ ___

_____ _____ __

IFL ZDUULYPVX TU MLNIF, ZT IFNI JK IFL XYNBL

___ _____ __ _____,

__ ____ __ ___ _____

TU XTM FL HPXFI INZIL MLNIF UTY LSLYKTVL.

__ ___ __ _____ _____

_____ ___ _____.

FLJYLEZ 2:9

_____ 2:9

PUZZLE 17: (AND JUSTICE, SO THAT)

XZT K DVYP RDZAPO DKJ, CDVC DP JVI RZJJVOW

___ _ ____ _____ ___,

____ __ ___ _____

DKA RDKHWTPO VOW DKA DZMAPDZHW VXCPT

___ _____ ___ ___

_____ _____

DKJ CZ QPPG CDP UVI ZX CDP HZTW LI WZKOB

___ __ ____ ___ ___ __

___ ____ __ _____

TKBDCPZMAOPAA VOW NMACKRP, AZ CDVC CDP

_____ ___

_____, __ ____ ___

HZTW JVI LTKOB CZ VLTVDVJ UDVC DP DVA

____ ___ _____ __

_____ ____ __ ___

GTZJKAPW DKJ."

_____ ___."

BPOPAKA 18:19

_____ 18:19

PUZZLE 18: (CASTS OUT FEAR.)

JIGHG BP OL XGFH BO ZLTG, WKJ MGHXGAJ

_ _ _ _ _   _ _   _ _   _ _ _ _   _ _   _ _ _ _,

_ _ _   _ _ _ _ _ _ _

ZLTG AFPJP LKJ XGFH. XLH XGFH IFP JL SL VBJI

_ _ _ _   _ _ _ _ _   _ _ _   _ _ _ _.   _ _ _

_ _ _ _   _ _ _   _ _   _ _   _ _ _ _

MKOBPIEGOJ, FOS VILGTGH XGFHP IFP OLJ

_ _ _ _ _ _ _ _ _ _ _,   _ _ _   _ _ _ _ _ _ _

_ _ _ _ _   _ _ _   _ _'_

WGGO MGHXGAJGS BO ZLTG.

_ _ _ _   _ _ _ _ _ _ _ _ _   _ _   _ _ _ _.

1 DLIO 4:18
1 _ _ _ _ 4:18

PUZZLE 19: (AWAIT A SAVIOR,)

QIF PIK WRFRJHYCDRE RC RY DHSUHY, SYV

___ ___ _____ __

__ _____, ___

AKPT RF ZH SZSRF S CSURPK, FDH OPKV BHCIC

____ __ __ _____ _

_____, ___ ____ _____

WDKRCF, ZDP ZROO FKSYCAPKT PIK OPZOG

_____, ___ ____

_____ ___ _____

QPVG FP QH ORXH DRC MOPKRPIC QPVG, QG

____ __ __ ____ ___

_____ ____, __

FDH EPZHK FDSF HYSQOHC DRT HUHY FP

___ _____ ____ _____

___ ____ __

CIQBHWF SOO FDRYMC FP DRTCHOA.

_____ ___ _____ __

_____.

EDROREERSYC 3:20–21

_____ 3:20–21

PUZZLE 20: (MAN, LEST YOU)

USBO HN YIROHEPXRM VRCX S USH KRLOH CN

____ __ _____ ____

_ ___ _____ __

SHKOI,

_____,

HNI KN VRCX S VISCXYGJ USH,

___ __ ____ _ _____

___,

JOPC ZNG JOSIH XRP VSZP

____ ___ _____ ___ ____

SHE OHCSHKJO ZNGIPOJY RH S PHSIO.

___ _____ _____

__ _ _____.

MINLOIFP 22:24–25

_, _____ 22:24–25

PUZZLE 21: (HIS WILL HE HEARS)

VRF GMTL TL GMN IZRQTFNRIN GMVG UN MVDN

___ ____ __ ___

_____ ____ __ ____

GZUVSF MTH, GMVG TQ UN VLA VRKGMTRO

_____ ___, ____ __ __

___ _____

VIIZSFTRO GZ MTL UTWW MN MNVSL YL. VRF TQ

_____ __ ___ ____ __

_____ __. ___ __

UN ARZU GMVG MN MNVSL YL TR UMVGNDNS UN

__ ____ ____ __ _____ __

__ _____ __

VLA, UN ARZU GMVG UN MVDN GMN SNPYNLGL

___, __ ____ ____ __ ____

___ _____

GMVG UN MVDN VLANF ZQ MTH.

____ __ ____ _____ __

___.

1 EZMR 5:14–15
1 __ __ __ __ 5:14–15

PUZZLE 22: (BEFORE OUTSIDERS)

GJL KV GTFPOQ KV MPUQ CDPQKMN, GJL KV

___ __ _____ __ ____

_____, ___ __

ZPJL NVDO VBJ GHHGPOT, GJL KV BVOW BPKR

____ ____ ___ _____,

___ __ ____ ____

NVDO RGJLT, GT BQ PJTKODIKQL NVD, TV KRGK

____ _____, __ __

_____ ___, __ ____

NVD ZGN BGMW FOVFQOMN SQHVOQ

___ ___ ____ _____

_____

VDKTPLQOT GJL SQ LQFQJLQJK VJ JV VJQ.

_____ ___ __

_____ __ __ ___.

1 KRQTTGMVJPGJT 4:11–12

1 __ __ __ __ __ __ __ __ __ __ __ __ __ 4:11–12

PUZZLE 23: (IS FITTING IN THE)

GRNOE, EIPQRC CS WSIH FIEPLZYE, LE RE

_____, _____ __ ____

_____, __ __

JRCCRZB RZ CFO XSHY. FIEPLZYE, XSNO WSIH

_____ __ ___ ____.

_____, ____ ____

GRNOE, LZY YS ZSC PO FLHEF GRCF CFOQ.

_____, ___ __ ___ __

_____ ____ ____.

TFRXYHOZ, SPOW WSIH VLHOZCE RZ

_____, ____ ____

_____ __

ONOHWCFRZB, JSH CFRE VXOLEOE CFO XSHY.

_____, ___ ____

_____ ___ ____.

JLCFOHE, YS ZSC VHSNSAO WSIH TFRXYHOZ,

_____, __ ___ _____

____ _____,

XOEC CFOW POTSQO YRETSIHLBOY.

____ ____ _____

_____.

TSXSEERLZE 3:18–21

_____ 3:18–21

PUZZLE 24: (SEES IN SECRET)

RIH XCYB GMI AUFY HM HCY BYYKG, KM BMH

___ _____ ___ ____ __ ___

_____, __ ___

DYH GMIQ DYLH CWBK TBMX XCWH GMIQ
QUACH

___ _____ ____ ____ ____

____ ____ _____

CWBK UV KMUBA, VM HCWH GMIQ AUFUBA ZWG

____ __ _____, __ ____

____ _____ ___

RY UB VYEQYH. WBK GMIQ LWHCYQ XCM VYYV

__ __ _____. ___ ____

_____ ___ ____

UB VYEQYH XUDD QYXWQK GMI.

__ _____ ____ _____

___.

ZWHHCYX 6:3–4

_____ 6:3–4

GE JDR KE RKH BJOPT SGTUKC, BZV LGC JTP

__ ___ __ ___ _____

_____, ___ ___ ___

QKU, SLK QGNZT QZDZXKHTBR VK JBB SGVLKHV

___, ___ _____

_____ __ ___

_____

XZFXKJOL, JDU GV SGBB YZ QGNZD LGC. YHV

_____, ___ __ ____ __

_____ ___. ___

BZV LGC JTP GD EJGVL, SGVL DK UKHYVGDQ,

___ ___ ___ __ _____,

____ __ _____,

EKX VLZ KDZ SLK UKHYVT GT BGPZ J SJNZ KE

___ ___ ___ ___ _____

__ ____ _ ____ __

VLZ TZJ VLJV GT UXGNZD JDU VKTTZU YR VLZ

___ ___ ____ __ _____

___ _____ __ ___

SGDU.

____.

IJCZT 1:5–6

_____ 1:5–6

PUZZLE 26: (SUBJECT ALL)

VFZ JFK ACZCYRSQWCO CQ CS WRPTRS, PSX

___ ___ _____ __

__ _____, ___

HKJG CZ NR PNPCZ P QPTCJK, ZWR IJKX LRQFQ

____ __ __ _____ _

_____, ___ ____ _____

AWKCQZ, NWJ NCII ZKPSQHJKG JFK IJNIB VJXB

_____, ___ ____

_____ ___ _____

____

ZJ VR ICDR WCQ MIJKCJFQ VJXB, VB ZWR OJNRK

__ __ ____ ___ _____

____, __ ___ _____

ZWPZ RSPVIRQ WCG RTRS ZJ QFVLRAZ PII

____ _____ ___ ____ __

_____ ___

ZWCSMQ ZJWCGQRIH.

_____ __ _____.

OWCICOOCPSQ 3:20–21

_____ 3:20–21

PUZZLE 27: (ONE WILL LIFT)

RBT KSI PIRRIS RDKO TOI, PIVKFQI RDIU DKJI K

___ ___ _____ ____ ___,

_____ ____ ____ _

ETTM SIBKSM GTS RDINS RTNW. GTS NG RDIU

____ _____ ___ _____

____. ___ __ ____

GKWW, TOI BNWW WNGR FA DNQ GIWWTB. PFR

____, ___ ____ ____ __

___ _____. ___

BTI RT DNL BDT NQ KWTOI BDIO DI GKWWQ
KOM

__ ___ ___ __ _____

____ __ _____ ___

DKQ OTR KOTRDIS RT WNGR DNL FA!

___ ___ _____ __ ____

___ __!

IVVWIQNKQRIQ 4:9–10

_____ 4:9–10

PUZZLE 28: (SOLD FOR A PENNY)

DXZ BVR RCV EODXXVCE EVFG LVX D OZBBQ?

___ ___ ___ _____

____ ___ _ _____?

DBG BVR VBZ VL RMZP CYFF LDFF RV RMZ

___ ___ ___ __ ____ ____

____ __ ___

HXVTBG DODXR LXVP QVTX LDRMZX. STR ZIZB

_____ _____ ____ ____

_____. ___ ____

RMZ MDYXE VL QVTX MZDG DXZ DFF BTPSZXZG.

___ _____ __ ____ ____

___ ___ _____.

LZDX BVR, RMZXZLVXZ; QVT DXZ VL PVXZ IDFTZ

____ ___, _____; ___

___ __ ____ _____

RMDB PDBQ EODXXVCE.

____ ____ _____.

PDRRMZC 10:29–31

_____ 10:29–31

PUZZLE 29: (YOUR MIGHT, FOR)

UGQBTRTX IWNX GQSK ZHSKE BW KW, KW HB

_ _ _ _ _ _ _ _ _   _ _ _ _   _ _ _ _

_ _ _ _   _ _   _ _,   _ _   _ _

UHBG IWNX LHAGB, ZWX BGTXT HE SW UWXJWX

_ _ _ _   _ _ _ _   _ _ _ _ _,   _ _ _

_ _ _ _ _   _ _   _ _   _ _ _ _   _ _

BGWNAGB WX JSWUDTKAT WX UHEKWL HS

_ _ _ _ _ _ _   _ _   _ _ _ _ _ _ _ _   _ _

_ _ _ _ _ _   _ _

EGTWD, BW UGHFG IWN QXT AWHSA.

_ _ _ _ _,   _ _   _ _ _ _ _   _ _ _   _ _ _

_ _ _ _ _.

TFFDTEHQEBTE 9:10

_ _ _ _ _ _ _ _ _ _ _ _ 9:10

PUZZLE 30: (AND SUBMISSIVE)

LMRWS ULJWI MXDWUXTWYSW FL GW

_____ _____ _____

___ __ __

SWNWSWIF XI GWCYNXLS, ILF TMYIRWSWST LS

_____ __ _____,

___ _____ __

TMYNWT FL JEZC UXIW. FCWPYSW FL FWYZC

_____ __ ____ ____. ____

___ __ _____

UCYF XT ALLR, YIR TL FSYXI FCW PLEIA ULJWI FL

____ __ ____, ___ __

_____ ___ _____ _____ __

MLNW FCWXS CETGYIRT YIR ZCXMRSWI, FL GW

____ _____ _____ ___

_____, __ __

TWMQ-ZLIFSLMMWR, OESW, ULSDXIA YF CLJW,

____-_____, ____,

_____ __ ____,

DXIR, YIR TEGJXTTXNW FL FCWXS LUI CETGYIRT,

____, ___ _____ __

_____ ___ _____

FCYF FCW ULSR LQ ALR JYP ILF GW SWNXMWR.

____ ___ ____ __ ___ ___
___ __ _____.

FXFET 2:3–5
_____ 2:3–5

PUZZLE 31: (AND GOOD HOPE)

LBO ZPX BNE UBEF KHINI WGEMID GMZIHUV, PLF

___ ___ ___ ____ _____
_____ _____, ___

SBF BNE VPDGHE, OGB UBQHF NI PLF SPQH NI

___ ___ _____, ___ _____
__ ___ ____ __

HDHELPU WBZVBED PLF SBBF GBAH DGEBNSG

_____ _____ ___
____ ____ _____

SEPWH, WBZVBED XBNE GHPEDI PLF HIDPTUMIG

_____, _____ ____
_____ ___ _____

DGHZ ML HQHEX SBBF OBEC PLF OBEF.

____ __ _____ ____ ____
___ ____.

2 DGHIIPUBLMPLI 2:16–17
2 _____ 2:16–17

PUZZLE 32: (APPEARED, BRINGING)

USX MTO KXPGO SU KSL TPB PRROPXOL,

___ ___ _____ __ ___ ___

_____,

EXVWKVWK BPCHPMVSW USX PCC ROSRCO,

_____ _____ ___

___ _____,

MXPVWVWK JB MS XOWSJWGO JWKSLCVWOBB

_____ __ __ _____

_____

PWL FSXCLCZ RPBBVSWB, PWL MS CVHO BOCU-

___ _____ _____,

___ __ _____ ____-

GSWMXSCCOL, JRXVKTM, PWL KSLCZ CVHOB VW

_____, _____, ___

_____ _____ __

MTO RXOBOWM PKO, FPVMVWK USX SJX

___ _____ ___, _____

___ ___

ECOBBOL TSRO, MTO PRROPXVWK SU MTO

_____ ____, ___

_____ __ ___

KCSXZ SU SJX KXOPM KSL PWL BPHVSX IOBJB

_ _ _ _ _ _ _ _ _ _ _ _ _ _ _ _ _ _

_ _ _ _ _ _ _ _ _ _ _ _ _ _

GTXVBM,

_ _ _ _ _ _,

MVMJB 2:11–13

_ _ _ _ _ _ 2:11–13

The nearer I approach to the end of my pilgrimage, the clearer is the evidence of the divine origin of the Bible, and the grandeur and sublimity of God's remedy for fallen man are more appreciated, and the future is illumined with hope and joy.
—Samuel Morse, inventor of the Morse Code telegraph system.
The first message he transmitted was "What hath God wrought!"
(from Numbers 23:23)

PUZZLE 33: (WHO BELIEVE: IN)

HSR PUIQI QEBSQ MEVV HAAGTZHSJ PUGQI MUG

___ _____ _____ ____

_____ _____ ___

CIVEILI: ES TJ SHTI PUIJ MEVV AHQP GOP

_____: __ __ ____ ____

____ ____ ___

RITGSQ; PUIJ MEVV QZIHN ES SIM PGSBOIQ; PUIJ

_____; ____ ____ _____

__ ___ _____; ____

MEVV ZEAN OZ QIYZISPQ MEPU PUIEY UHSRQ;

____ ____ __ _____

____ _____ _____;

HSR ED PUIJ RYESN HSJ RIHRVJ ZGEQGS, EP

___ __ ____ _____ ___

_____ _____, __

MEVV SGP UOYP PUIT; PUIJ MEVV VHJ PUIEY

____ ___ ____ ____; ____

____ ___ _____

UHSRQ GS PUI QEAN, HSR PUIJ MEVV YIAGLIY."

_____ __ ___ ____, ___

____ ____ _____."

THYN 16:17–18

__ __ __ __ 16:17–18

PUZZLE 34: (YOUR GOD, OBEYING)

Y TGHH EUGJUC GCW UGBRE RM KYRCUOO

_ ____ _____ ___ _____

__ _____

GSGYCOR AML RMWGA, REGRY EGJU OUR

_____ ___ _____, ____

_ ____ ___

IUPMBU AML HYPU GCW WUGRE, IHUOOYCS

_____ ___ ____ ___

_____, _____

GCW TLBOU. REUBUPMBU TEMMOU HYPU, REGR

___ _____. _____

_____ ____, ____

AML GCW AMLB MPPOXBYCS DGA HYJU, HMJYCS

___ ___ ____ _____

___ _____, _____

REU HMBW AMLB SMW, MIUAYCS EYO JMYTU

___ ____ ____ ___,

_____ ___ _____

GCW EMHWYCS PGOR RM EYD, PMB EU YO

___ _____ ____ __ ___,

___ __ __

AMLB HYPU GCW HUCSRE MP WGAO, REGR AML

____ ____ ___ _____ __

____, ____ ___

DGAWKUHHYC REU HGCW REGR REU HMBW

___ _____ __ ___ ____

____ ___ ____

OKMBU RM AMLB PGREUBO, RM GIBGEGD, RM

_____ __ ____ _____, __

_____, __

YOGGT, GCW RM ZGTMI, RM SYJU REUD."

_____, ___ __ _____, __

____ ____."

WULRUBMCMDA 30:19–20

_____ 30:19–20

PUZZLE 35: (WITH ANYONE IN)

NSC CMS CMKSG QE NEQVSU BCSTN, PXC

___ ___ _____ __ _____

_____, ___

UTCMSU NSC MKA NTPEU, REKQV MEQSBC HEUI

_____ ___ ___ _____,

_____ _____ ____

HKCM MKB EHQ MTQRB, BE CMTC MS ATZ MTDS

____ ___ ___ _____, __

____ __ ___ ____

BEASCMKQV CE BMTUS HKCM TQZEQS KQ QSSR.

_____ __ _____ ____

__ ___ __ ____.

SOMSBKTQB 4:28

_____ 4:28

PUZZLE 36: (THE MERCIES OF)

M VNNTVD GU PUX GETITCUIT, HIUGETIB, HP
GET

__ _____ __ ___

_____, _____, __

___

WTIYMTB UC FUL, GU NITBTQG PUXI HULMTB
VB

_____ __ ___, __

_____ ____ _____ __

V DMKMQF BVYIMCMYT, EUDPVQL
VYYTNGVHDT

__ _____ _____, ____

___ _____

GU FUL, REMYE MB PUXI BNMIMGXVD RUIBEMN.

__ ___, _____ __ ____

_____ _____.

IUWVQB 12:1

_____ 12:1

PUZZLE 37: (FLESH, THAT MEANS)

EB EP OG ZXFZH ZTYZQBXBEWI XIJVWYZ

__ __ __ _____

_____ ___ ____

BVXB E SEKK IWB AZ XB XKK XPVXOZJ, AMB

____ _ ____ ___ __ __ ___

_____, ___

BVXB SEBV LMKK QWMHXFZ IWS XP XKSXGP

____ ____ ____ _____

___ __ _____

QVHEPB SEKK AZ VWIWHZJ EI OG AWJG,

_____ ____ __ _____

__ __ ____,

SVZBVZH AG KELZ WH AG JZXBV. LWH BW OZ BW

_____ __ ___ __ __

_____. ___ __ __ __

KERZ EP QVHEPB, XIJ BW JEZ EP FXEI. EL E XO

____ __ _____, ___ __

___ __ ____. __ _ __

BW KERZ EI BVZ LKZPV, BVXB OZXIP LHMEBLMK

__ ____ __ ___ _____,

____ _____ _____

KXAWH LWH OZ. GZB SVEQV E PVXKK QVWWPZ E

_____ ___ __. ___ _____ _

_____ _____ _

QXIIWB BZKK.

_____ ____.

YVEKEYYEXIP 1:20–22

_____ 1:20–22

PUZZLE 38: (THAT I GO)

"ZGQ SJQ PJAH DGLHQI OG QHJAOZGX.

"___ ___ ____ _____ __

_____.

OGZTGEG TS UJX; OGZTGEG LZIJ TS YG. TS YP

_____ __ ___; _____

____ __ __. __ __

RLQDGH'I DJAIG LHG YLSP HJJYI. TR TQ VGHG

_____'_ _____ ___ ____

_____. __ __ ____

SJQ IJ, VJAZX T DLEG QJZX PJA QDLQ T UJ QJ

___ __, _____ _ _____ ____

___ ____ _ __ __

WHGWLHG L WZLMG RJH PJA? LSX TR T UJ LSX

_____ _ _____ ___ __?

___ __ _ __ ___

WHGWLHG L WZLMG RJH PJA, T VTZZ MJYG

_____ _ _____ ___ ___,

_ ____ ____

LULTS LSX VTZZ QLFG PJA QJYPIGZR, QDLQ

_____ ___ ____ ____ ___

__ _____, ____

VDGHG T LY PJAYLP OG LZIJ.

_____ _ __ ___ ___ __

____.

BJDS 14:1–3

__ __ __ __ 14:1–3

PUZZLE 39: (HIM, SAYING, I WILL)

HXG LRICQG, H QRDRU MHOR EC INO HXG

___ _____, _ _____ ____

__ ___ ___

TXRQE LRWCUR INO, AHZNXB, "QCUG, NW ZCK

_____ _____ ___, _____,

"____, __ ___

YNQQ, ZCK MHX OHTR OR MQRHX." HXG VRAKA

____, ___ ___ ____ __

_____." ___ _____

AEUREMIRG CKE INA IHXG HXG ECKMIRG INO,

_____ ___ ___ ____

___ _____ ___,

AHZNXB, "N YNQQ; LR MQRHX." HXG

_____, "_ ____; __ _____."

___

NOORGNHERQZ INA QRDUCAZ YHA MQRHXARG.

_____ ___ _____

___ _____.

OHEEIRY 8:2–3

_____ 8:2–3

PUZZLE 40: (THEM, AND HEALING)

ZS EPX, OC LFFCXFURC FP ZS APVBE;

__ ___, __ _____ __
__ _____;

UXJYUXC SPKV CLV FP ZS ELSUXIE.

_____ ____ ___ __ __
_____.

YCF FNCZ XPF CEJLMC DVPZ SPKV EUINF;

___ ____ ___ _____ ____
____ _____;

TCCM FNCZ AUFNUX SPKV NCLVF.

____ ____ _____ ____
_____.

DPV FNCS LVC YUDC FP FNPEC ANP DUXB FNCZ,

___ ____ ___ ____ __
_____ ___ ____ ____,

LXB NCLYUXI FP LYY FNCUV DYCEN.

___ _____ __ ___ _____
_____.

TCCM SPKV NCLVF AUFN LYY RUIUYLXJC,

____ ____ _____ ____ ___
_____,

DPV DVPZ UF DYPA FNC EMVUXIE PD YUDC.

___ _____ __ ____ ___

__ __ ____ __ ____.

MVPRCVOE 4:20–23

_____ 4:20–23

PUZZLE 41: (FAILED OF ALL)

"LPANNAO LA VDA PSIO UDS DMN YEBAZ IANV VS

" _____ __ ___ ____ ___

___ _____ ____ __

DEN HASHPA ENIMAP, MWWSIOEZY VS MPP

___ _____ _____,

_____ __ ___

VDMV DA HISQENAO. ZSV SZA USIO DMN

____ __ _____. ___ ___

____ ___

RMEPAO SR MPP DEN YSSO HISQENA, UDEWD DA

_____ __ ___ ___ ____

_____, _____ __

NHSJA LX QSNAN DEN NAIBMZV.

_____ __ _____ ___

_____.

1 JEZYN 8:56

1 _____ 8:56

PUZZLE 42: (PEACE, AND WITH)

KFLVIX DV DOK UGLAV GFL JLQVSK

‗‗‗‗‗‗ ‗‗ ‗‗‗ ‗‗‗‗‗ ‗‗‗
‗‗‗‗‗‗

OAM BOLLQVM GFL KGLLGCK;

‗‗‗ ‗‗‗‗‗‗‗ ‗‗‗ ‗‗‗‗‗‗‗;

XVZ CV VKZVVWVM DQW KZLQBYVA,

‗‗‗ ‗‗ ‗‗‗‗‗‗‗‗ ‗‗‗
‗‗‗‗‗‗‗‗,

KWQZZVA UX JGM, OAM OSSIQBZVM.

‗‗‗‗‗‗‗ ‗‗ ‗‗‗, ‗‗‗
‗‗‗‗‗‗‗‗‗.

UFZ DV COK CGFAMVM SGL GFL

‗‗‗ ‗‗ ‗‗‗ ‗‗‗‗‗‗‗ ‗‗‗
‗‗‗

ZLOAKJLVKKQGAK;

‗‗‗‗‗‗‗‗‗‗‗‗‗‗;

DV COK BLFKDVM SGL GFL QAQPFQZQVK;

‗‗ ‗‗‗ ‗‗‗‗‗‗‗ ‗‗‗ ‗‗‗
‗‗‗‗‗‗‗‗‗;

FTGA DQW COK ZDV BDOKZQKVWVAZ ZDOZ

‗‗‗‗ ‗‗‗ ‗‗‗ ‗‗‗
‗‗‗‗‗‗‗‗‗‗‗‗ ‗‗‗‗

ULGFJDZ FK TVOBV,

———————— —— —————,

OAM CQZD DQK KZLQTVK CV OLV DVOIVM.

——— ———— ——— ——————— ——

——— ——————.

QKOQOD 53:4–5

—— —— —— 53:4–5

PUZZLE 43: (EVIL DISEASES OF)

TDL VEH FPWL JAFF VTYH TJTB OWPN BPX TFF

——— ——— ———— ———— ————

———— ———— ——— ———

RAMYDHRR, TDL DPDH PO VEH HUAF LARHTRHR

———————— , ——— ———— —— ———

———— —————————

PO HZBQV, JEAME BPX YDHJ, JAFF EH ADOFAMV

—— —————— , —————— ——— ———— ,

———— —— —————————

PD BPX, CXV EH JAFF FTB VEHN PD TFF JEP ETVH

—— ——— , ——— —— ———— ———

———— —— ——— ——— ————

BPX.

— — —.

LHXVHWPDPNB 7:15

— — — — — — — — — — — — 7:15

PUZZLE 44: (ALL HIS STATUTES)

"YN WUQ TYBB ZYBYLXFKBW BYHKXF

"— — — — — — — — — — — — — — — — — — —
— — — — — —

KU KIX RUYDX UN KIX BUAZ WUQA LUZ, CFZ ZU

— — — — — — — — — — — — — — — —
— — — — — — —, — — — — —

KICK TIYDI YH AYLIKYF IYH XWXH, CFZ LYRX

— — — — — — — — — — — — — —
— — — — — — —, — — — — — — —

XCA KU IYH DUGGCFZGXFKH CFZ SXXV CBB IYH

— — — — — — — — — — — — — — — — — — —
— — — — — — — — — — — — —

HKCKQKXH, Y TYBB VQK FUFX UN KIX

ZYHXCHXH

— — — — — — — —, — — — — — — — — — — —
— — — — — — — — — — —

UF WUQ KICK Y VQK UF KIX XLWVKYCFH, NUA Y

— — — — — — — — — — — — — — — — — —
— — — — — — — — — —, — — — —

CG KIX BUAZ, WUQA IXCBXA."

__ __ ___ ____, ____ _____."

XMUZQH 15:26

__ __ __ __ __ __ 15:26

PUZZLE 45: (BUT THE PATH OF)

RJG GQT HSGQ EA GQT XUKQGTEJM UM VULT

___ ___ ____ __ ___

_____ __ ____

GQT VUKQG EA YSNF,

___ _____ __ ____,

NQUWQ MQUFTM RXUKQGTX SFY RXUKQGTX

_____ _____ _____

___ _____

JFGUV AJVV YSP.

_____ ____ ___.

GQT NSP EA GQT NUWLTY UM VULT YTTH

___ ___ __ ___ _____ __

____ ____

YSXLFTMM;

_____;

GQTP YE FEG LFEN EITX NQSG GQTP MGJORVT.

____ __ ___ ____ ____

____ ____ _____.

HXEITXRM 4:18–19

_____ 4:18–19

PUZZLE 46: (ALL YOUR HEART, AND)

OKFQO MR OGI XBKA UMOG JXX PBFK GIJKO,

_____ __ ___ ____ ____

___ ____ _____,

JRA AB RBO XIJR BR PBFK BUR FRAIKQOJRAMRD.

___ __ ___ ____ __ ____

___ _____.

MR JXX PBFK UJPQ JWERBUXIADI GML,

__ ___ ____ ____

_____ ___,

JRA GI UMXX LJEI QOKJMDGO PBFK TJOGQ.

___ __ ____ ____

_____ ____ _____.

TKBCIKSQ 3:5–6

_____ 3:5–6

PUZZLE 47: (BETTER THAN THAT)

PE C PGA KRGK KRTXT CP BEKRCBU ZTKKTX

__ _ ___ ____ _____ __
_____ _____

KRGB KRGK G SGB PREDJL XTQECVT CB RCP

____ ____ _ ___ _____
_____ __ ___

AEXN, YEX KRGK CP RCP JEK. ARE VGB ZXCBU

____, ___ ____ __ ___ ___.
___ ___ _____

RCS KE PTT ARGK ACJJ ZT GYKTX RCS?

___ __ ___ ____ ____ __
_____ ___?

TVVJTPCGPKTP 3:22

_____ 3:22

PUZZLE 48: (FOR YOU, LEST)

HO RVM IEZF OVMWA IVWFR, FEN VWSR FWVMDI

__ ___ ____ _____ _____,
___ ____ _____

OVG RVM,

___ ___,

SFCN RVM IEZF RVMG OHSS VO HN EWA ZVQHN
HN.

____ ___ ____ ____ ____
__ __ ___ _____ __.

SFN RVMG OVVN JF CFSAVQ HW RVMG

___ ____ ____ __ _____
__ ____

WFHDIJVG'C IVMCF,

_____'_ _____,

SFCN IF IEZF IHC OHSS VO RVM EWA IENF RVM.

____ __ ____ ___ ____ __
___ ___ ____ ___.

XGVZFGJC 25:16–17
_____ 25:16–17

PUZZLE 49: (COMES INTO YOUR)

SW TVNLXIVM, MXNA EN UKVLGKDGLW KM WNB

__ __ _____, ____ __

_____ __ ___

XNDH LXI JKGLX GE NBV DNVH RIMBM YXVGML,

____ ___ _____ __ ___

____ _____ _____,

LXI DNVH NJ FDNVW. JNV GJ K SKE AIKVGEF K

___ ____ __ _____. ___ __

_ ___ _____ _

FNDH VGEF KEH JGEI YDNLXGEF YNSIM GELN

____ ____ ___ ____

_____ _____ ____

WNBV KMMISTDW, KEH K UNNV SKE GE
MXKTTW

____ _____, ___ _ ____

___ __ _____

YDNLXGEF KDMN YNSIM GE, KEH GJ WNB UKW

_____ ____ _____ __,

___ __ ___ ___

KLLIELGNE LN LXI NEI AXN AIKVM LXI JGEI

_____ __ ___ ___ ___

_____ ___ ____

YDNLXGEF KEH MKW, "WNB MGL XIVI GE K FNNH

_____ ___ ___, "___

___ ____ __ _ ____

UDKYI," AXGDI WNB MKW LN LXI UNNV SKE, "WNB

_____," _____ ___ ___ __

___ ____ ___, "___

MLKEH NZIV LXIVI," NV, "MGL HNAE KL SW JIIL,"

_____ ____ _____," __, "___

____ __ __ ____,"

XKZI WNB ENL LXIE SKHI HGMLGEYLGNEM KSNEF

____ ___ ___ ____ ____

_____ _____

WNBVMIDZIM KEH TIYNSI RBHFIM AGLX IZGD

_____ ___ _____

_____ ____ ____

LXNBFXLM?

_____?

RKSIM 2:1–4

_____ 2:1–4

PUZZLE 50: (IF TWO OR THREE)

BOBRF R EBZ SC ZCL, RM STC CM ZCL BOIAA CF

_____ _ ___ __ ___, __ ___

__ ___ _____ __

ABISU BGCLS BFZSURFO SUAZ BEN, RS TRKK GA

_____ _____ _____

____ ___, __ ____ __

QCFA MCI SUAJ GZ JZ MBSUAI RF UABDAF. MCI

____ ___ ____ __ __

_____ __ _____. ___

TUAIA STC CI SUIAA BIA OBSUAIAQ RF JZ FBJA,

_____ ___ __ _____ ___

_____ __ __ ____,

SUAIA BJ R BJCFO SUAJ."

_____ __ _ _____ ____."

JBSSUAT 18:19–20

_____ 18:19–20

PUZZLE 51: (AS WE ARE, YET)

ETL ON FT ATM JKZN K JVYJ SLVNRM OJT VR

___ __ __ ___ ____ _ ____

_____ ___ __

QAKIGN MT RCWSKMJVUN OVMJ TQL

‗ ‗ ‗ ‗ ‗ ‗   ‗ ‗   ‗ ‗ ‗ ‗ ‗ ‗ ‗ ‗ ‗ ‗

‗ ‗ ‗ ‗   ‗ ‗ ‗

ONKDANRRNR, IQM TAN OJT VA NZNLC LNRSNXM

‗ ‗ ‗ ‗ ‗ ‗ ‗ ‗ ‗ ‗,   ‗ ‗ ‗   ‗ ‗ ‗   ‗ ‗ ‗

‗ ‗   ‗ ‗ ‗ ‗ ‗   ‗ ‗ ‗ ‗ ‗ ‗ ‗

JKR INNA MNWSMNF KR ON KLN, CNM OVMJTQM

‗ ‗ ‗   ‗ ‗ ‗ ‗   ‗ ‗ ‗ ‗ ‗ ‗ ‗   ‗ ‗   ‗ ‗

‗ ‗ ‗,   ‗ ‗ ‗   ‗ ‗ ‗ ‗ ‗ ‗ ‗

RVA. GNM QR MJNA OVMJ XTAEVFNAXN FLKO

‗ ‗ ‗.   ‗ ‗ ‗   ‗ ‗   ‗ ‗ ‗ ‗   ‗ ‗ ‗ ‗

‗ ‗ ‗ ‗ ‗ ‗ ‗ ‗ ‗ ‗   ‗ ‗ ‗ ‗

ANKL MT MJN MJLTAN TE YLKXN, MJKM ON WKC

‗ ‗ ‗ ‗   ‗ ‗   ‗ ‗ ‗   ‗ ‗ ‗ ‗ ‗ ‗   ‗ ‗

‗ ‗ ‗ ‗ ‗,   ‗ ‗ ‗ ‗   ‗ ‗   ‗ ‗ ‗

LNXNVZN WNLXC KAF EVAF YLKXN MT JNGS VA

‗ ‗ ‗ ‗ ‗ ‗ ‗   ‗ ‗ ‗ ‗ ‗   ‗ ‗ ‗   ‗ ‗ ‗ ‗

‗ ‗ ‗ ‗ ‗   ‗ ‗   ‗ ‗ ‗ ‗   ‗ ‗

MVWN TE ANNF.

‗ ‗ ‗ ‗   ‗ ‗   ‗ ‗ ‗ ‗.

JNILNOR 4:15–16

‗ ‗ ‗ ‗ ‗ ‗ ‗ 4:15–16

PUZZLE 52: (IN THE PRESENT AGE,)

CAK RGI FKBEI AC FAQ GBT BZZIBKIQ, NKSHFSHF

___ ___ _____ __ ___ ___

_____, _____

TBMOBRSAH CAK BMM ZIAZMI, RKBSHSHF LT RA

_____ ___ ___

_____, _____ __ __

KIHALHEI LHFAQMSHITT BHQ XAKMQMP

_____ _____

___ _____

ZBTTSAHT, BHQ RA MSOI TIMC-EAHRKAMMIQ,

_____, ___ __ ____

____-_____,

LZKSFGR, BHQ FAQMP MSOIT SH RGI ZKITIHR

_____, ___ _____ _____

__ ___ _____

BFI, XBSRSHF CAK ALK NMITTIQ GAZI, RGI

___, _____ ___ ___

_____ ____, ___

BZZIBKSHF AC RGI FMAKP AC ALK FKIBR FAQ

_____ __ ___ _____

__ ___ _____ ___

BHQ TBOSAK UITLT EGKSTR,

——— ——————— ————— ——————,

RSRLT 2:11–13

— — — — — 2:11–13

PUZZLE 53: (CHRIST THROUGH)

BEWCWKUCW, QZPSW TW ERMW LWWP

——————————, —————— —— ————
————

OHQBZKZWI LV KRZBE, TW ERMW GWRSW TZBE

—————————— —— ——————, ——
————— ————— ————

FUI BECUHFE UHC JUCI OWQHQ SECZQB.

——— ——————— ——— ————
————— ——————.

BECUHFE EZD TW ERMW RJQU ULBRZPWI

———————— ——— —— ———— ————
————————

RSSWQQ LV KRZBE ZPBU BEZQ FCRSW ZP TEZSE

—————— —— ————— ————
————— —————— —— —————

TW QBRPI, RPI TW CWOUZSW ZP EUGW UK BEW

—— ———————, ——— —— ————————
—— ————— —— ———

FJUCV UK FUI.

_ _ _ _ _ _ _ _ _ _.

CUDRPQ 5:1–2

_ _ _ _ _ _ 5:1–2

PUZZLE 54: (THAT THERE WOULD BE A)

QUZ JQ DWROR CETO SHUSWRDO VEPR CUZQ

_ _ _ _ _ _ _ _ _ _ _ _ _ _

_ _ _ _ _ _ _ _ _ _ _ _ _ _ _ _

NHUP ARHXOEYRP DU EQDJUVW. EQC UQR UN

_ _ _ _ _ _ _ _ _ _ _ _ _ _ _

_ _ _ _ _ _ _. _ _ _ _ _ _ _ _

DWRP QEPRC EFEGXO ODUUC XS EQC

_ _ _ _ _ _ _ _ _ _ _ _ _ _ _ _ _ _ _ _

_ _ _ _ _

NUHRDUYC GT DWR OSJHJD DWED DWRHR

_ _ _ _ _ _ _ _ _ _ _ _ _ _ _ _ _ _ _

_ _ _ _ _ _ _ _ _

ZUXYC GR E FHRED NEPJQR UBRH EYY DWR

_ _ _ _ _ _ _ _ _ _ _ _ _ _ _ _ _ _ _ _

_ _ _ _ _ _ _ _ _ _

ZUHYC (DWJO DUUL SYEVR JQ DWR CETO UN

_ _ _ _ _ (_ _ _ _ _ _ _ _ _ _ _ _ _ _ _

_ _ _ _ _ _ _ _ _

VYEXCJXO). OU DWR CJOVJSYRO CRDRHPJQRC,

_ _ _ _ _ _ _ _). _ _ _ _ _

_ ,

RBRHTUQR EVVUHCJQF DU WJO EGJYJDT, DU

_ _ _ _ _ _ _ _ _ _ _ _ _ _ _ _ _ _ _

_ _ _ _ _ _ _ _ _ _ , _ _

ORQC HRYJRN DU DWR GHUDWRHO YJBJQF JQ

_ _ _ _ _ _ _ _ _ _ _ _ _ _ _

_ _ _ _ _ _ _ _ _ _ _ _ _ _ _

AXCRE. EQC DWRT CJC OU, ORQCJQF JD DU

_ _ _ _ . _ _ _ _ _ _ _ _ _ _ _ ,

_ _ _ _ _ _ _ _ _ _ _

DWR RYCRHO GT DWR WEQC UN GEHQEGEO

_ _ _ _ _ _ _ _ _ _ _ _ _ _ _ _ _

_ _ _ _ _ _ _ _ _

EQC OEXY.

_ _ _ _ _ _ _ .

EVDO 11:27–30

_ _ _ _ 11:27–30

PUZZLE 55: (WE WILL NOT FEAR)

ISB KR SZG GOXZIO FWB RMGOWIMU,

___ __ ___ _____ ___

_____,

F QOGEYGOROWM UOJY KW MGSZNJO.

_ ____ _____ ____ __

_____.

MUOGOXSGO AO AKJJWSM XOFG MUSZIU MUO

_____ __ ____ ___

____ _____ ___

OFGMU IKQOR AFE,

_____ _____ ___,

MUSZIU MUO CSZWMFKWR NO CSQOB KWMS

_____ ___ _____ __

_____ ____

MUO UOFGM SX MUO ROF,

___ _____ __ ___ ___,

YRFJC 46:1–2

_____ 46:1–2

PUZZLE 56: (HE SAID, "TRULY)

FYKRK ASSQYU RE PTU KPB OWY DXJW

_ _ _ _ _   _ _ _ _ _ _ _   _ _   _ _ _   _ _ _

_ _ _   _ _ _ _

EROOXTM OWYXD MXGOK XTOS OWY

_ _ _ _ _ _ _   _ _ _ _ _   _ _ _ _ _

_ _ _ _   _ _ _

SGGYDXTM HSV, PTUWY KPB P ESSD BXUSB

_ _ _ _ _ _ _ _   _ _ _,   _ _ _   _ _   _ _ _

_   _ _ _ _   _ _ _ _ _

ERO XT OBS KNPAA JSEEYD JSXTK. PTUWY

_ _ _   _ _   _ _ _   _ _ _ _ _   _ _ _ _ _

_ _ _ _ _.   _ _ _   _ _

KPXU, "ODRAC, X OYAA CSR, OWXK ESSD BXUSB

_ _ _ _,   "_ _ _ _ _,   _   _ _ _ _   _ _ _,

_ _ _ _   _ _ _ _ _   _ _ _ _ _

WPK ERO XT NSDY OWPT PAA SG OWYN. GSD

_ _ _   _ _ _   _ _   _ _ _ _   _ _ _ _   _ _ _

_ _   _ _ _ _.   _ _ _

OWYC PAA JSTODXHROYU SRO SG OWYXD

_ _ _ _   _ _ _   _ _ _ _ _ _ _ _ _ _ _

_ _ _   _ _   _ _ _ _ _

PHRTUPTJY, HRO KWY SRO SGWYD ESZYDOC

_ _ _ _ _ _ _ _ _ _,   _ _ _   _ _ _   _ _ _   _ _

_ _ _   _ _ _ _ _ _ _

ERO XT PAA KWY WPU OS AXZY ST."

___ __ ___ ___ ___ __

____ __."

ARQY 21:1–4

____ 21:1–4

PUZZLE 57: (YOU. NO LONGER DO)

"GPOR OR JZ QXJJULBJILG, GPUG ZXA DXYI XLI

"____ __ __ _____,

____ ___ ____ ___

ULXGPIS UR O PUYI DXYIB ZXA. ESIUGIS DXYI

_____ __ _ ____ _____

___. _____ ____

PUR LX XLI GPUL GPOR, GPUG RXJIXLI DUZ BXFL

___ __ ___ ____ ____,

____ _____ ___ ____

POR DOTI TXS POR TSOILBR. ZXA USI JZ TSOILBR

___ ____ ___ ___ _____.

___ ___ __ _____

OT ZXA BX FPUG O QXJJULB ZXA. LX DXLEIS BX O

__ ___ __ ____ _ _____

___. __ _____ __ _

QUDD ZXA RISYULGR, TXS GPI RISYULG BXIR

____ ___ _____, ___

___ _____ ____

LXG MLXF FPUG POR JURGIS OR BXOLE; HAG O

___ ____ ____ ___ _____

__ _____; ___ _

PUYI QUDDIB ZXA TSOILBR, TXS UDD GPUG O

____ _____ ___ _____,

___ ___ ____ _

PUYI PIUSB TSXJ JZ TUGPIS O PUYI JUBI MLXFL

____ _____ ____ __

_____ _ ____ ____ _____

GX ZXA.

__ ___.

WXPL 15:12–15

__ __ __ __ 15:12–15

PUZZLE 58: (WITH MY RIGHTEOUS)

XLBZ VFU, XFZ II BJ OHUR NFW;

____ ___, ___ _ __ ____

__ _;

IL VFU CHDJBNLC, XFZ H BJ NFWZ QFC;

__ ___ _____, ___ _ __

____ ___;

H OHKK DUZLVQURLV NFW, H OHKK RLKS NFW,

_ ____ _____ ___, _

____ ____ ___,

H OHKK WSRFKC NFW OHUR JN ZHQRULFWD

__ _____ _____ ___ ____

___ _____

ZHQRU RBVC.

_____ ____.

XFZ H, URL KFZC NFWZ QFC,

___ _, ___ ____ ____ ___,

RFKC NFWZ ZHQRU RBVC;

____ ____ _____ ____;

HU HD H ORF DBN UF NFW, "XLBZ VFU,

__ __ _ ___ ___ __ ___,

"____ ___,

H BJ URL FVL ORF RLKSD NFW."

_ __ ___ ___ ___ _____

___."

HDBHBR 41:10,13

_____ 41:10, 13

PUZZLE 59: (SERVED IN THE)

QHM WP WF WG NYWE WH SRXU NSNG FR

___ __ __ __ ____ __ ____

____ __

GNUYN FBN ERUM, ZBRRGN FBWG MQS KBRD

_____ ___ ____, _____

____ ___ ____

SRX KWEE GNUYN, KBNFBNU FBN VRMG SRXU

___ ____ _____, _____

___ ____ ____

PQFBNUG GNUYNM WH FBN UNVWRH CNSRHM

_____ _____ __ ___

_____ _____

FBN UWYNU, RU FBN VRMG RP FBN QDRUWFNG

___ _____, __ ___ ____ __

___ _____

WH KBRGN EQHM SRX MKNEE. CXF QG PRU DN

__ _____ ____ ___ ____.

___ __ ___ __

QHM DS BRXGN, KN KWEE GNUYN FBN ERUM."

___ __ _____, __ ____

_____ ___ ____."

ARGBXQ 24:15

_____ 24:15

PUZZLE 60: (SONS, AND GIVE YOUR)

"SUFH HIMH SUP BROX RV URHSH, SUP ERX RV

"_ _ _ _   _ _ _ _   _ _ _   _ _ _ _   _ _

_ _ _ _ _,   _ _ _   _ _ _   _ _

NHOIPB, SR IBB SUP PLNBPH QURJ N UIGP HPTS

_ _ _ _ _,   _ _   _ _ _   _ _ _   _ _ _ _ _

_ _ _ _   _   _ _ _ _   _ _ _ _

NTSR PLNBP VORJ DPOFHIBPJ SR ZIZMBRT:

_ _ _ _   _ _ _ _ _   _ _ _ _

_ _ _ _ _ _ _ _ _   _ _   _ _ _ _ _ _ _:

ZFNBX URFHPH ITX BNGP NT SUPJ; WBITS

_ _ _ _ _   _ _ _ _ _ _ _   _ _ _   _ _ _ _   _ _

_ _ _ _;   _ _ _ _ _

EIOXPTH ITX PIS SUPNO WORXFKP. SICP QNGPH

_ _ _ _ _ _ _   _ _ _   _ _ _   _ _ _ _ _

_ _ _ _ _ _ _.   _ _ _ _ _   _ _ _ _ _

ITX UIGP HRTH ITX XIFEUSPOH; SICP QNGPH VRO

_ _ _   _ _ _ _   _ _ _ _   _ _ _

_ _ _ _ _ _ _ _ _   _ _ _ _   _ _ _ _ _

_ _ _

MRFO HRTH, ITX ENGP MRFO XIFEUSPOH NT

_ _ _ _   _ _ _ _,   _ _ _   _ _ _ _   _ _ _ _

_ _ _ _ _ _ _ _ _   _ _

JIOONIEP, SUIS SUPM JIM ZPIO HRTH ITX

__ __ __ __ __ __ __ __, __ __ __ __ __ __ __ __ __ __ __

__ __ __ __ __ __ __ __ __ __ __

XIFEUSPOH; JFBSNWBM SUPOP, ITX XR TRS

__ __ __ __ __ __ __ __ __; __ __ __ __ __ __ __ __ __

__ __ __ __ __, __ __ __ __ __ __ __ __

XPKOPIHP.

__ __ __ __ __ __ __ __.

DPOPJNIU 29:4–6

__ __ __ __ __ __ __ __ 29:4–6

VOCABULARY BUILDER — "WISDOM"

1. The quality or state of being wise; knowledge of what is true or right coupled with just judgment as to action; sagacity, discernment, or insight.
2. Scholarly knowledge or learning

CRYPTOGRAM SOLUTIONS

PUZZLE 1:
So those who received his word were baptized, and there were added that day about three thousand souls. Acts 2:41

PUZZLE 2:
So we, though many, are one body in Christ, and individually members one of another. Romans 12:5

PUZZLE 3:
Fear not, for I am with you; be not dismayed, for I am your God; I will strengthen you, I will help you, I will uphold you with my righteous right hand. Isaiah 41:10

PUZZLE 4:
Now when they saw the boldness of Peter and John, and perceived that they were uneducated, common men, they were astonished. And they recognized that they had been with Jesus. Acts 4:13

PUZZLE 5:
But the Lord God helps me; therefore I have not been disgraced; therefore I have set my face like a flint, and I know that I shall not be put to shame. Isaiah 50:7

PUZZLE 6:
And let us consider how to stir up one another to love and good works, not neglecting to meet together, as is the habit of some, but encouraging one another, and all the more as you see the Day drawing near. Hebrews 10:24–25

PUZZLE 7:
For he who sanctifies and those who are sanctified all have one source. That is why he is not ashamed to call them brothers,

saying, "I will tell of your name to my brothers; in the midst of the congregation I will sing your praise." Hebrews 2:11–12

PUZZLE 8:
But in the following instructions I do not commend you, because when you come together it is not for the better but for the worse. For, in the first place, when you come together as a church, I hear that there are divisions among you. And I believe it in part, 1 Corinthians 11:17–18

PUZZLE 9:
There is nothing better for a person than that he should eat and drink and find enjoyment in his toil. This also, I saw, is from the hand of God, for apart from him who can eat or who can have enjoyment? Ecclesiastes 2:24–25

PUZZLE 10:
Do not be afraid of sudden terror or of the ruin of the wicked, when it comes, for the Lord will be your confidence and will keep your foot from being caught. Proverbs 3:25–26

PUZZLE 11:
If a brother or sister is poorly clothed and lacking in daily food, and one of you says to them, "Go in peace, be warmed and filled," without giving them the things needed for the body, what good is that? James 2:15–16

PUZZLE 12:
Honor the Lord with your wealth and with the firstfruits of all your produce; then your barns will be filled with plenty, and your vats will be bursting with wine. Proverbs 3:9–10

PUZZLE 13:
The Lord does not let the righteous go hungry, but he thwarts the craving of the wicked. A slack hand causes poverty, but the hand of the diligent makes rich. Proverbs 10:3–4

PUZZLE 14:

For to me to live is Christ, and to die is gain. If I am to live in the flesh, that means fruitful labor for me. Yet which I shall choose I cannot tell. I am hard pressed between the two. My desire is to depart and be with Christ, for that is far better. But to remain in the flesh is more necessary on your account. Philippians 1:21–24

PUZZLE 15:

And Jesus returned in the power of the Spirit to Galilee, and a report about him went out through all the surrounding country. And he taught in their synagogues, being glorified by all. And he came to Nazareth, where he had been brought up. And as was his custom, he went to the synagogue on the Sabbath day, and he stood up to read. Luke 4:14–16

PUZZLE 16:

But we see him who for a little while was made lower than the angels, namely Jesus, crowned with glory and honor because of the suffering of death, so that by the grace of God he might taste death for everyone. Hebrews 2:9

PUZZLE 17:

For I have chosen him, that he may command his children and his household after him to keep the way of the Lord by doing righteousness and justice, so that the Lord may bring to Abraham what he has promised him." Genesis 18:19

PUZZLE 18:

There is no fear in love, but perfect love casts out fear. For fear has to do with punishment, and whoever fears has not been perfected in love. 1 John 4:18

PUZZLE 19:

But our citizenship is in heaven, and from it we await a Savior, the Lord Jesus Christ, who will transform our lowly body to be like his glorious body, by the power that enables him even to subject all things to himself. Philippians 3:20–21

PUZZLE 20:
Make no friendship with a man given to anger, nor go with a wrathful man, lest you learn his ways and entangle yourself in a snare. Proverbs 22:24–25

PUZZLE 21:
And this is the confidence that we have toward him, that if we ask anything according to his will he hears us. And if we know that he hears us in whatever we ask, we know that we have the requests that we have asked of him. 1 John 5:14–15

PUZZLE 22:
And to aspire to live quietly, and to mind your own affairs, and to work with your hands, as we instructed you, so that you may walk properly before outsiders and be dependent on no one. 1 Thessalonians 4:11–12

PUZZLE 23:
Wives, submit to your husbands, as is fitting in the Lord. Husbands, love your wives, and do not be harsh with them. Children, obey your parents in everything, for this pleases the Lord. Fathers, do not provoke your children, lest they become discouraged. Colossians 3:18–21

PUZZLE 24:
But when you give to the needy, do not let your left hand know what your right hand is doing, so that your giving may be in secret. And your Father who sees in secret will reward you. Matthew 6:3–4

PUZZLE 25:
If any of you lacks wisdom, let him ask God, who gives generously to all without reproach, and it will be given him. But let him ask

in faith, with no doubting, for the one who doubts is like a wave of the sea that is driven and tossed by the wind. James 1:5–6

PUZZLE 26:

But our citizenship is in heaven, and from it we await a Savior, the Lord Jesus Christ, who will transform our lowly body to be like his glorious body, by the power that enables him even to subject all things to himself. Philippians 3:20–21

PUZZLE 27:

Two are better than one, because they have a good reward for their toil. For if they fall, one will lift up his fellow. But woe to him who is alone when he falls and has not another to lift him up! Ecclesiastes 4:9–10

PUZZLE 28:

Are not two sparrows sold for a penny? And not one of them will fall to the ground apart from your Father. But even the hairs of your head are all numbered. Fear not, therefore; you are of more value than many sparrows. Matthew 10:29–31

PUZZLE 29:

Whatever your hand finds to do, do it with your might, for there is no work or thought or knowledge or wisdom in Sheol, to which you are going. Ecclesiastes 9:10

PUZZLE 30:

Older women likewise are to be reverent in behavior, not slanderers or slaves to much wine. They are to teach what is good, and so train the young women to love their husbands and children, to be self-controlled, pure, working at home, kind, and submissive to their own husbands, that the word of God may not be reviled. Titus 2:3–5

PUZZLE 31:
Now may our Lord Jesus Christ himself, and God our Father, who loved us and gave us eternal comfort and good hope through grace, comfort your hearts and establish them in every good work and word. 2 Thessalonians 2:16–17

PUZZLE 32:
For the grace of God has appeared, bringing salvation for all people, training us to renounce ungodliness and worldly passions, and to live self-controlled, upright, and godly lives in the present age, waiting for our blessed hope, the appearing of the glory of our great God and Savior Jesus Christ, Titus 2:11–13

PUZZLE 33:
And these signs will accompany those who believe: in my name they will cast out demons; they will speak in new tongues; they will pick up serpents with their hands; and if they drink any deadly poison, it will not hurt them; they will lay their hands on the sick, and they will recover." Mark 16:17–18

PUZZLE 34:
I call heaven and earth to witness against you today, that I have set before you life and death, blessing and curse. Therefore choose life, that you and your offspring may live, loving the Lord your God, obeying his voice and holding fast to him, for he is your life and length of days, that you may dwell in the land that the Lord swore to your fathers, to Abraham, to Isaac, and to Jacob, to give them." Deuteronomy 30:19–20

PUZZLE 35:
Let the thief no longer steal, but rather let him labor, doing honest work with his own hands, so that he may have something to share with anyone in need. Ephesians 4:28

PUZZLE 36:

I appeal to you therefore, brothers, by the mercies of God, to present your bodies as a living sacrifice, holy and acceptable to God, which is your spiritual worship. Romans 12:1

PUZZLE 37:

It is my eager expectation and hope that I will not be at all ashamed, but that with full courage now as always Christ will be honored in my body, whether by life or by death. For to me to live is Christ, and to die is gain. If I am to live in the flesh, that means fruitful labor for me. Yet which I shall choose I cannot tell. Philippians 1:20–22

PUZZLE 38:

"Let not your hearts be troubled. Believe in God; believe also in me. In my Father's house are many rooms. If it were not so, would I have told you that I go to prepare a place for you? And if I go and prepare a place for you, I will come again and will take you to myself, that where I am you may be also. John 14:1–3

PUZZLE 39:

And behold, a leper came to him and knelt before him, saying, "Lord, if you will, you can make me clean." And Jesus stretched out his hand and touched him, saying, "I will; be clean." And immediately his leprosy was cleansed. Matthew 8:2–3

PUZZLE 40:

My son, be attentive to my words; incline your ear to my sayings. Let them not escape from your sight; keep them within your heart. For they are life to those who find them, and healing to all their flesh. Keep your heart with all vigilance, for from it flow the springs of life. Proverbs 4:20–23

PUZZLE 41:

"Blessed be the Lord who has given rest to his people Israel, according to all that he promised. Not one word has failed of all his good promise, which he spoke by Moses his servant. 1 Kings 8:56

PUZZLE 42:

Surely he has borne our griefs and carried our sorrows; yet we esteemed him stricken, smitten by God, and afflicted. But he was wounded for our transgressions; he was crushed for our iniquities; upon him was the chastisement that brought us peace, and with his stripes we are healed. Isaiah 53:4–5

PUZZLE 43:

And the Lord will take away from you all sickness, and none of the evil diseases of Egypt, which you knew, will he inflict on you, but he will lay them on all who hate you. Deuteronomy 7:15

PUZZLE 44:

"If you will diligently listen to the voice of the Lord your God, and do that which is right in his eyes, and give ear to his commandments and keep all his statutes, I will put none of the diseases on you that I put on the Egyptians, for I am the Lord, your healer." Exodus 15:26

PUZZLE 45:

But the path of the righteous is like the light of dawn, which shines brighter and brighter until full day. The way of the wicked is like deep darkness; they do not know over what they stumble. Proverbs 4:18–19

PUZZLE 46:

Trust in the Lord with all your heart, and do not lean on your own understanding. In all your ways acknowledge him, and he will make straight your paths. Proverbs 3:5–6

PUZZLE 47:

So I saw that there is nothing better than that a man should rejoice in his work, for that is his lot. Who can bring him to see what will be after him? Ecclesiastes 3:22

PUZZLE 48:

If you have found honey, eat only enough for you, lest you have your fill of it and vomit it. Let your foot be seldom in your neighbor's house, lest he have his fill of you and hate you. Proverbs 25:16–17

PUZZLE 49:

My brothers, show no partiality as you hold the faith in our Lord Jesus Christ, the Lord of glory. For if a man wearing a gold ring and fine clothing comes into your assembly, and a poor man in shabby clothing also comes in, and if you pay attention to the one who wears the fine clothing and say, "You sit here in a good place," while you say to the poor man, "You stand over there," or, "Sit down at my feet," have you not then made distinctions among yourselves and become judges with evil thoughts? James 2:1–4

PUZZLE 50:

Again I say to you, if two of you agree on earth about anything they ask, it will be done for them by my Father in heaven. For where two or three are gathered in my name, there am I among them." Matthew 18:19–20

PUZZLE 51:

For we do not have a high priest who is unable to sympathize with our weaknesses, but one who in every respect has been tempted as we are, yet without sin. Let us then with confidence draw near to the throne of grace, that we may receive mercy and find grace to help in time of need. Hebrews 4:15–16

PUZZLE 52:

For the grace of God has appeared, bringing salvation for all people, training us to renounce ungodliness and worldly passions, and to live self-controlled, upright, and godly lives in the present age, waiting for our blessed hope, the appearing of the glory of our great God and Savior Jesus Christ, Titus 2:11–13

PUZZLE 53:

Therefore, since we have been justified by faith, we have peace with God through our Lord Jesus Christ. Through him we have also obtained access by faith into this grace in which we stand, and we rejoice in hope of the glory of God. Romans 5:1–2

PUZZLE 54:

Now in these days prophets came down from Jerusalem to Antioch. And one of them named Agabus stood up and foretold by the Spirit that there would be a great famine over all the world (this took place in the days of Claudius). So the disciples determined, everyone according to his ability, to send relief to the brothers living in Judea. And they did so, sending it to the elders by the hand of Barnabas and Saul. Acts 11:27–30

PUZZLE 55:

God is our refuge and strength, a very present help in trouble. Therefore we will not fear though the earth gives way, though the mountains be moved into the heart of the sea, Psalm 46:1–2

PUZZLE 56:

Jesus looked up and saw the rich putting their gifts into the offering box, and he saw a poor widow put in two small copper coins. And he said, "Truly, I tell you, this poor widow has put in more than all of them. For they all contributed out of their abundance, but she out of her poverty put in all she had to live on." Luke 21:1–4

PUZZLE 57:

"This is my commandment, that you love one another as I have loved you. Greater love has no one than this, that someone lay down his life for his friends. You are my friends if you do what I command you. No longer do I call you servants, for the servant does not know what his master is doing; but I have called you friends, for all that I have heard from my Father I have made known to you. John 15:12–15

PUZZLE 58:

Fear not, for I am with you; be not dismayed, for I am your God; I will strengthen you, I will help you, I will uphold you with my righteous right hand.
For I, the Lord your God, hold your right hand; it is I who say to you, "Fear not, I am the one who helps you." Isaiah 41:10,13

PUZZLE 59:

And if it is evil in your eyes to serve the Lord, choose this day whom you will serve, whether the gods your fathers served in the region beyond the River, or the gods of the Amorites in whose land you dwell. But as for me and my house, we will serve the Lord." Joshua 24:15

PUZZLE 60:

"Thus says the Lord of hosts, the God of Israel, to all the exiles whom I have sent into exile from Jerusalem to Babylon: Build houses and live in them; plant gardens and eat their produce. Take wives and have sons and daughters; take wives for your sons, and give your daughters in marriage, that they may bear sons and daughters; multiply there, and do not decrease. Jeremiah 29:4–6

Part Two
CROSSWORD PUZZLES

PUZZLE 1: THE APOSTLES

1	2	3		4	5	6	7		8	9	10	11
12				13					14			
15				16					17			
		18	19					20				
21	22						23					
24					25				26	27	28	
29				30	31				32			
33				34					35			
			36				37	38				
39	40	41				42						
43					44					45	46	47
48					49					50		
51					52					53		

ACROSS

1. Anointing chrism in many churches
4. " . . . no blood be ___ for him" (Exodus 22:2)
8. "I judge not mine own ___" (1 Corinthians 4:3)
12. Actress Thurman
13. Do some roadwork
14. Biblical no-no
15. " . . . and one ___ for a burnt offering" (Leviticus 16:5)
16. ___ in the bush
17. " . . . let no man ___ his bones" (2 Kings 23:18)
18. An apostle
21. Pass by, as time
23. Number of Commandments
24. Resounding approval, from Alicante
25. Wide shoe width
26. Smog-watching grp.
29. Two of the apostles

33. Dir. from Atlanta to Baltimore
34. Office holders
35. Singer Jagger
36. ___ moment's notice
37. Cavern or river edges
39. Two of the apostles
43. Designer Cassini
44. " . . . and vessels of brass and

___, . . . " (Joshua 6:19)
45. Snooze
48. "Zip-___-Doo-Dah"
49. Space beginning
50. Apr. 15th advisor
51. Dudley Do-Right's love
52. ___ Fein
53. Slippery as an ___

DOWN

1. Lord's Prayer opener
2. John Denver's "Thank God ___ Country Boy"
3. Scold sharply
4. Bandies words
5. Literary Bret
6. "Well, Did You ___?" (Porter tune)
7. Took a stripe from
8. An apostle
9. Dead Sea region
10. " . . . to ___ the Lord your god" (Deuteronomy 11:13)
11. "Then ___ one of the seraphims unto me" (Isaiah 6:6)
19. " . . . blackbirds baked in ___"
20. Actor Cobb
21. Network owned by Disney

22. Property restriction
25. "Nun" has two
26. Cardinal's title, with "Your"
27. Legendary actor Gregory
28. Seeks some answers
30. Woman in a Beatles' song
31. Biblical high priest (Acts 23:2)
32. In the center of
36. Divine messenger
37. Tennis star Borg
38. Talk nonstop
39. ___ of Arc
40. "Ye ___ Curiosity Shoppe"
41. " . . . lifted up his ___ against me" (Psalm 41:9)
42. Three, in Germany
46. King Kong, e.g.
47. Good buddy

PUZZLE 2: THE GOOD BOOKS

1	2	3	4		5	6	7		8	9	10
11					12				13		
14					15				16		
17				18		19		20			
21				22	23					24	
25			26					27	28		
			29				30				
31	32	33				34			35	36	37
38				39	40				41		
42			43					44	45		
46				47		48		49			
50				51				52			
53				54				55			

ACROSS

1. "___ ye well" (Acts 15:29)
5. Nightwear, for short
8. Muscle spasm
11. Sea of ___ (Black Sea arm)
12. "What was that?"
13. Work together in harmony
14. Large books, such as the Bible
15. Eisenhower's monogram
16. Great report card marks
17. Tehran native

19. OT book
21. "And the ___ of the place asked him of his wife" (Genesis 26:7)
22. Dictation whiz
24. "Thou shalt not ___ of it" (Genesis 3:17)
25. Frees from doubt
27. "Thou shalt truly ___ all the increase of thy seed" (Deuteronomy 14:22)

29. "And Jotham ___ away, and fled" (Judges 9:21)
30. " . . . and God saw that it ___ good" (Genesis 1:12)
31. "Keep me as the ___ of the eye" (Psalm 17:8)
34. The tax gatherer
38. They make up qts.
39. Sierra ___
41. "Thou art my battle ___ and weapons of war" (Jeremiah 51:20)
42. Book with only one chapter

44. Delight in the taste of
46. Actress Falana
47. "For Me and My ___"
49. Miami county
50. " . . . and took a ___ out of the flock" (1 Samuel 17:34)
51. " . . . neither ___ one to another" (Leviticus 19:11)
52. Faulkner's "Requiem for ___"
53. Tiebreaking periods, for short
54. Geologic period
55. Ship's pole

DOWN

1. Our Lady of ___ (Portuguese shrine)
2. Islands off Portugal
3. NT book
4. Neck-and-neck
5. Doctorate deg.
6. OT book
7. Bishop or Martin
8. China shop purchase
9. OT book
10. "To be discreet, ___, keepers at home" (Titus 2:5)
13. Astronaut Jemison
18. One led by Moses out of Egypt
20. Draws musical symbols

23. "___ cubits shall be the length of a board" (Exodus 26:16)
26. Home page address, e.g.
28. Column ending
30. Pallid
31. Historic NASA mission
32. Small WWII craft
33. OT book
34. Angora's coat
35. Capital of Cuba
36. OT book
37. "As if that ___ enough . . . "
40. "Doth the ___ mount up at thy command" (Job 39:27)
43. Pat on
45. First Edenite
48. Pastoral place

PUZZLE 3: THE WORD

1	2	3	4	5		6	7	8		9	10	11
12						13				14		
15						16		17				
		18		19				20				
21	22			23				24				
25			26		27		28					
29				30			31			32	33	34
			35			36			37			
38	39	40				41		42		43		
44					45				46			
47				48				49			50	51
52				53				54				
55				56				57				

ACROSS

1. Jacob's wife and namesakes
6. Mass robe
9. Waitress in Mel's Diner
12. Chance for a hit
13. Bapt. or Episc.
14. He ran from Sodom
15. ___ firma
16. "Paul also and Barnabas continued in ___" (Acts 15:35)
18. With hands on hips
20. Zap in the microwave
21. ___ jongg
23. 502, to the Romans
24. Last word of some fairy tales
25. See 49-Across
27. Fall temporarily into sin
29. Prophet who anointed Saul and David as kings
31. Second name of Jacob
35. No longer in
37. He sank with the Scharnhorst

38. Well-suited to the task
41. H in New Testament Greek
43. Methuselah-like
44. Trio in Bethlehem
45. Tracts of wasteland
47. Devotional prayer commemorating the Annunciation

49. With 25-Across, devotional response
52. Suffix meaning "resident"
53. ___ carte
54. Words before pieces or the good
55. Character actor Beatty
56. Rabbit's foot
57. Wintry precipitation

DOWN

1. Back muscle, briefly
2. Summer, in Paris
3. "And ___ rose up early in the morning" (Genesis 21:14)
4. "___! The Herald Angels Sing"
5. Sedate
6. "For this Agar is mount Sinai in ___" (Galatians 4:25)
7. Big-jawed TV host
8. Sandwich order
9. Treat with disdain
10. English philosopher John
11. "And he stayed yet ___ seven days" (Genesis 8:10)
17. Deduces
19. " . . . and ground it in ___" (Numbers 11:8)
21. AWOL pursuers
22. "And the sons of Jether; Jephunneh, and Pispah, and ___" (1 Chronicles 7:38)

24. "And he found a new jawbone of an ___" (Judges 15:15)
26. BMW driver, maybe
28. Sculpture of the Virgin Mary and Jesus
30. "Thou shalt not ___ of it" (Genesis 3:17)
32. Peter, James or John
33. Sushi dish
34. "But God ___ the people about" (Exodus 13:18)
36. Playground attraction
38. At full force
39. *The Divine Comedy* poet
40. Urged (with "on")
42. Map book
45. Dance at a luau
46. Satan's abode
48. Once around the track
50. Multipurpose truck
51. Barfly

PUZZLE 4: OLD TESTAMENT BOOKS

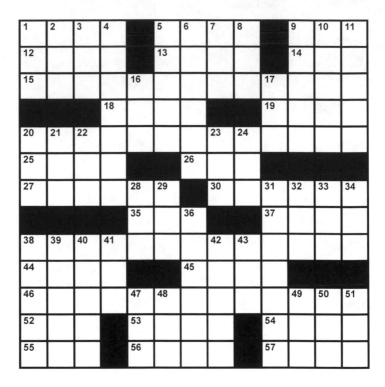

ACROSS

1. Water-to-wine town
5. " . . . and it shall be thy ___ " (Exodus 29:26)
9. Noah's son
12. Sensory stimulant
13. Together, in music
14. Honest President?
15. TWO OLD TESTAMENT BOOKS
18. "And God ___ the firmament" (Genesis 1:7)
19. "As an eagle stirreth up her ___ " (Deuteronomy 32:11)
20. TWO OLD TESTAMENT BOOKS
25. Jai ___
26. Drop of gel
27. Señor on the Sullivan show
30. Perfumed ointment
35. Spanish aunt
37. *Night* author Wiesel

38. TWO OLD TESTAMENT
    BOOKS
44. This, señor
45. Mythical queen of Carthage
46. TWO OLD TESTAMENT
    BOOKS

52. Actress Zadora
53. *Green Mansions* girl
54. OT BOOK
55. French possessive
56. Slangy snack
57. Lyricist Lorenz

DOWN

1. Runner Sebastian
2. Wood-dressing tool
3. " . . . will not fail thee, ___
   forsake thee" (Joshua 1:5)
4. Biblical language
5. Washington Zoo animal
6. Number next to a plus sign
7. Wish one could take back
8. ___-Mex food
9. Mythical hell
10. Mistreatment
11. River of Thrace or hostess
    Perle
16. Checkup sound
17. Yoko ___
20. " . . . with the ___ of an
    ass . . ." (Judges 15:16)
21. Grand ___ Opry
22. One of the Bobbsey twins
23. Skip, as a stone on water
24. Cable station

28. LAX guesstimate
29. Go against God's
    commandments
31. Hanukkah centerpiece
32. 1996 Olympic torch lighter
33. "Ye shall not surely ___"
    (Genesis 3:4)
34. Serpentine swimmer
36. Uncle Fester or Morticia
38. WWII vehicles
39. Actor Davis
40. Kett and James
41. ___-di-dah
42. Leah's daughter
43. Say a bit more
47. Flying fish eater
48. Brazilian city
49. Actress Thurman
50. Rocky pinnacle
51. FDR's successor

PUZZLE 5: PARABLES

¹	²	³	⁴	■	⁵	⁶	⁷	■	⁸	⁹	¹⁰ ¹¹

ACROSS

1. Old Testament book
5. Prohibit
8. " . . . name of the ___ is called
   Wormwood" (Revelation 8:11)
12. Agitate
13. Ginger follower
14. Singer ___ Falana
15. Parable told in Luke 10:30–37
18. Prefix meaning "bone"
19. Amaze
20. Pencil stump

22. Polar home
26. "___ She Lovely"
29. Harness
32. ___ de Cologne
33. Parable told in Matthew
    25:31–46
36. "He maketh me to ___
    down in green . . . "
    (Psalm 23:2)
37. Change the decor
38. "You there!"

39. "He setteth an ___ darkness" (Job 28:3)
41. Necklace of flowers
43. Minor part of the world?
46. Haggard
50. Parable related in Luke 13:6–9
54. Frosted
55. Hockey Hall of Famer Bobby
56. Self-images

57. " . . . he should ___ the armies of the living God?" (1 Samuel 17:26)
58. "My beloved is like a ___ or a young hart" (Song of Solomon 2:9)
59. "Also he ___ forth a dove from him" (Genesis 8:8)

DOWN

1. Consequently
2. Where leopards get spotted
3. " . . . having faithful children not accused of ___ or unruly"
4. Firm, like pasta
5. Sheep shout?
6. "Sell that ye have, and give ___" (Luke 12:33)
7. ___ as a pin
8. David's weapon
9. Small child
10. Pie ___ mode
11. "And the servant ___ to meet her" (Genesis 24:17)
16. French coin
17. Feeling remorse
21. Scottish hillside
23. Pastures
24. Food grains
25. Kick out
26. "Be still, ye inhabitants of the ___" (Isaiah 23:2)

27. Leg part
28. "They that be whole ___ not a physician" (Matthew 9:12)
30. " . . . endureth to the ___ shall be saved" (Matthew 10:22)
31. Golden calf, e.g.
34. Ordinary writing
35. Narcotics
40. Late
42. "Or if he shall ask an ___, will he offer him a scorpion?"
44. "Are you ___ out?"
45. Early Michael Jackson hairdo
47. Encourage
48. Light gas
49. Pop quiz, for one
50. Make an offer
51. Excellent tennis serve
52. Ump's relative
53. Wrath

CROSSWORD PUZZLE SOLUTIONS

PUZZLE 1: THE APOSTLES

```
O I L   S H E D   S E L F
U M A   P A V E   I D O L
R A M   A R A M   M O V E
    B A R T H O L O M E W
E L A P S E   T E N
S I S I   E E E   E P A
P E T E R A N D J A M E S
N N E   I N S   M I C K
    A T A   B R I N K S
J O H N A N D J U D E
O L E G   I R O N   N A P
A D E E   A E R O   C P A
N E L L   S I N N   E E L
```

PUZZLE 3: THE WORD

```
L E A H S   A L B   F L O
A T B A T   R E L   L O T
T E R R A   A N T I O C H
    A K I M B O   N U K E
M A H   D I I   A F T E R
P R A Y   L A P S E
S A M U E L   I S R A E L
    P A S S E   S P E E
A D E P T   E T A   O L D
M A G I   H E A T H S
A N G E L U S   L E T U S
I T E   A L A   A L L T O
N E D   P A W   S L E E T
```

PUZZLE 2: THE GOOD BOOKS

```
F A R E   P J S   T I C
A Z O V   H U H   M E S H
T O M E   D D E   A A A A
I R A N I   G E N E S I S
M E N   S T E N O   E A T
A S S U R E S   T I T H E
    R A N   W A S
A P P L E   M A T T H E W
P T S   L E O N E   A X E
O B A D I A H   S A V O R
L O L A   G A L   D A D E
L A M B   L I E   A N U N
O T S   E R A   M A S T
```

PUZZLE 4: OLD TESTAMENT BOOKS

```
C A N A   P A R T   H A M
O D O R   A D U E   A B E
E Z R A A N D E X O D U S
    M A D E   N E S T
J O N A H A N D H O S E A
A L A I   D A B
W E N C E S   P O M A D E
    T I A   E L I E
J O E L A N D D A N I E L
E S T A   D I D O
E S T H E R A N D R U T H
P I A   R I M A   A M O S
S E S   N O S H   H A R T
```

PUZZLE 5: PARABLES

¹E	²Z	³R	⁴A	■	⁵B	⁶A	⁷N	■	⁸S	⁹T	¹⁰A ¹¹R

(Grid solution)

E	Z	R	A	■	B	A	N	■	S	T	A	R
R	O	I	L	■	A	L	E	■	L	O	L	A
G	O	O	D	S	A	M	A	R	I	T	A	N
O	S	T	E	O	■	S	T	U	N	■	■	■
■	■	N	U	B	■	■	I	G	L	O	O	
I	S	N	T	■	R	E	I	N	■	E	A	U
S	H	E	E	P	A	N	D	G	O	A	T	S
L	I	E	■	R	E	D	O	■	P	S	S	T
E	N	D	T	O	■	■	L	E	I	■	■	
■	■	A	S	I	A	■	G	A	U	N	T	
B	A	R	R	E	N	F	I	G	T	R	E	E
I	C	E	D	■	O	R	R	■	E	G	O	S
D	E	F	Y	■	R	O	E	■	S	E	N	T

Matthew Fontaine Maury was born in 1806. He was a renowned American astronomer, oceanographer, meteorologist, cartographer, and geologist. He earned the nicknames Pathfinder of the Seas and Father of Modern Oceanography. He published extremely extensive works on oceanography and was an expert on charting winds and ocean currents. He is credited with discovering pathways for ships at sea, which before him, were mere myths. But long before Matthew Fontaine Maury came along with his brilliant studies, several Bible passages alluded to "paths in the sea." Psalm 8:8 declares, "The fish of the sea that pass through the paths of the seas," and Isaiah 43:16 states, "Thus says the LORD, who makes a way in the sea and a path through the mighty waters."

Part Three
SUDOKU

How to Play Biblical Sudoku

Sudoku is one of the most popular games in the world. Playing requires no word, calculation, or arithmetic skills whatsoever. It is a simple game of placing numbers in squares using logic. These fun puzzles are solved worldwide by children and adults alike. But these forty puzzles have a unique biblical twist to them, as you'll soon learn after reviewing the rules.

Sudoku Objective

The objective of Sudoku is to fill in all the blank squares with a number from 1 to 9. Zero is never used. There are three very simple rules to follow:

Every **row** of 9 numbers must include all digits 1 through 9 without repeats in any order

Every **column** of 9 numbers must include all digits 1 through 9 without repeats in any order

Every 3 by 3 **subsection** of the 9 by 9 square must include all digits 1 through 9 without repeats in any order.

All Sudoku puzzles begin with a number of squares already filled in, making solving the puzzles possible through a little logic. As you fill in the blank squares correctly, options for the remaining squares are narrowed and it becomes easier and easier to fill them in. I've gone one step further. In each puzzle are three gray squares that correspond to the chapter and verse of a Bible Scripture listed. This can be a major clue for you as you solve these puzzles. Take your time and enjoy!

Colossians 2:19 states, "He has lost connection with the Head, from whom the whole body, supported and held together by its ligaments and sinews, grows as God causes it to grow." This verse explains that human growth emulates from the head. Many, many years later man discovered that the pituitary gland, or hypophysis, is an endocrine gland about the size of a pea, protruding off the bottom of the hypothalamus at the base of the brain. One of the primary functions of the pituitary gland is to promote growth in the human body.

PUZZLE 1

				9				3
8	5				4		9	
2			7			5		
3			9	6				
	6		2		8		5	
				4	1			9
		1			2			6
	4		3				2	8
9				1				

Clue:

1 Chronicles __ __ : __

Go and tell David my servant, Thus saith the Lord, Thou shalt not build me an house to dwell in.

PUZZLE 2

7			3	8		1		
			4					2
8				6		9	7	
	6	7				2		
			7		3			
		3				5	9	
	1	9		5				3
4					6			
		8		7	4			1

Clue:

1 John __ : __ __

And we have known and believed the love that God hath to us. God is love; and he that dwelleth in love dwelleth in God, and God in him.

PUZZLE 3

	9			7	1			
1			6	9	3		7	8
								5
				6	5		9	2
		3				4		
9	1		7	2				
7								
8	3		2	5	7			9
			8	3			2	

Clue:

Acts __ : __ __

And immediately there fell from his eyes as it had been scales: and he received sight forthwith, and arose, and was baptized.

PUZZLE 4

			9		3		6	
			7		2			3
	6			5				9
9		5	4				1	
3								6
	1				7	3		8
1				8			7	
7			6		5			
	9		3		1			

Clue:

Mark __ : __ __

When I brake the five loaves among five thousand, how many baskets full of fragments took ye up? They say unto him, Twelve.

PUZZLE 5

	4		6	9				
			4			8	5	6
		8			1			
	6			1		3		5
		2				9		
5		4	3				2	
			1			7		
7	9	6			2			
▒	▒	▒		7	9		4	

Clue:

Matthew __ __ : __

Then shall the kingdom of heaven be likened unto ten virgins, which took their lamps, and went forth to meet the bridegroom.

PUZZLE 6

4			7					
		6	4			7		9
			1				2	8
			6	3		1		
	4		9		2		5	
		2		7	4			
8	3				5			
9		5			1	2		
▒	▒	▒			7			3

Clue:

Psalm __ __ : __

Judge me, O LORD; for I have walked in mine integrity: I have trusted also in the LORD; therefore I shall not slide.

PUZZLE 7

	2			9		5		
5	1	8						
				2	6			3
7					8			
	5	1	6		9	2	8	
			4					6
1			7	3				
						7	2	9
		5		8			3	

Clue:

1 Samuel __ __ : __

And he said, Peaceably: I am come to sacrifice unto the LORD.

PUZZLE 8

3	1							
2			5	1				
	4					9		
8	7		4	5				2
		9	1		7	8		
1				3	9		5	7
		4					1	
				9	1			6
							3	9

Clue:

Leviticus __ __ : __

Ye shall eat your bread to the full, and dwell in your land safely.

PUZZLE 9

		9	8			4	6	3
	8							7
2		6						
	2			3	6			8
		7				5		
8			1	5			7	
						6		2
7			░	░	░		4	
1	6	4		9		7		

Clue:

Ephesians __ : __ __

Praying always with all prayer and supplication in the Spirit, and watching thereunto with all perseverance and supplication for all saints.

PUZZLE 10

	5				7		1	4
				2			5	
2	1			5			9	7
8					4			5
░	░	░		3				
7			6					9
9	3			4			7	1
	2			6				
4	8		9				2	

Clue:

Acts __ __ : __

And so were the churches established in the faith, and increased in number daily.

5		3	7			8	6	
		1		5				
9				6				
		8			4	6	1	
			▦	▦	▦			
	3	5	6			7		
				9				2
				7		1		
	9	6			2	5		7

Clue:

Deuteronomy __ : __ __

Go thou near, and hear all that the LORD our God shall say.

				6	4	3		
1			5	9		7	6	
					3		5	
		5			7	6		
	7		▦	▦	▦		9	
		4	3			8		
	2		4					
	4	3		1	2			7
		6	8	3				

Clue:

Deuteronomy __ __ : __

Blessed shalt thou be when thou comest in, and blessed shalt thou be when thou goest out.

PUZZLE 13

1		5			8	2	4	9
	2		5			8		
3	9							6
▓	▓	▓		3				
	7		1		5		2	
				6				
7							9	5
	4				3		7	
9	5	6	7			1		4

Clue:

1 Thessalonians __ : __ __

For ye, brethren, became followers of the churches of God which in Judaea are in Christ Jesus.

PUZZLE 14

9				4		3	5	
		3	7			8		
	1		6		3			
		1	▓	▓	▓		6	
3	4						9	8
	8				2			
			4		6		8	
		6			1	5		
	3	7		5				9

Clue:

Romans __ : __ __

For whom he did foreknow, he also did predestinate to be conformed to the image of his Son.

PUZZLE 15

Clue:

Romans __ : __ __

Even so now yield your members servants to righteousness unto holiness.

PUZZLE 16

Clue:

Hebrews __ : __ __

I will be merciful to their unrighteousness, and their sins and their iniquities will I remember no more.

PUZZLE 17

	4			5				
		4			6			
	5	2			3	4		1
▓	▓	▓	4			1	8	
			8		6			
	4	6		9				
1		5	9			8	7	
		9			2			
			6			3		

Clue:

Psalm __ __ : __

The voice of the LORD is upon the waters: the God of glory thundereth: the LORD is upon many waters.

PUZZLE 18

		4		2	3	5		
								3
	8		1	5	7			9
	3		9					
7				6				4
					5		1	
1			4	7	9		6	
8			▓	▓	▓			
		9	5	1		7		

Clue:

Psalm __ __ : __

Surely goodness and mercy shall follow me all the days of my life: and I will dwell in the house of the LORD for ever.

PUZZLE 19

		5					3	2
8		6			1			
			3		5		8	
2	9			7		3		
		1		4			6	9
	1		6		9	░		
			2			5		8
9	5					1		

Clue:

Psalm __ __ : __

Though an host should encamp against me, my heart shall not fear.

PUZZLE 20

7					6			1
	6			2				
1	5	2	9					
		1		4		5		
5								2
		4		8		3		
░	░	░			2	7	4	8
				6			2	
8			5					6

Clue:

Psalm __ __ : __

For thou, O God, hast heard my vows: thou hast given me the heritage of those that fear thy name.

PUZZLE 21

	3				7		4	1
4		2	6					5
				9			3	
5						9		6
		4				3		
3		8	▓	▓				7
	4			8				
1					5	8		9
8	6		9				7	

Clue:

Acts __ : __ __

And they gave forth their lots; and the lot fell upon Matthias; and he was numbered with the eleven apostles.

PUZZLE 22

			2			5	6	
			3		8		9	
▓	▓	▓		9		7	4	
9		5					2	
		8			1			
	3					4		7
2	5		1					
	8		5		7			
	4	7			6			

Clue:

Mark __ : __ __

And he sighed deeply in his spirit, and saith, Why doth this generation seek after a sign?

PUZZLE 23

Clue:
Luke __ : __ __

Then he took the five loaves and the two fishes, and looking up to heaven, he blessed them, and brake, and gave to the disciples to set before the multitude.

PUZZLE 24

Clue:
Ecclesiastes __ : __ __

Wisdom is better than weapons of war.

PUZZLE 25

7	8		3	5				
6								8
	1		7					
1					3			4
	6	4				7	9	
2			1					5
					2		8	
8								6
				9	1		2	7

Clue:

1 Corinthians __ __ : __

For he that speaketh in an unknown tongue speaketh not unto men, but unto God.

PUZZLE 26

				4		1		
4					3	7		2
3			1		6			
	5			3		9		
	6						1	
		9		8			7	
			3		4			8
5		3	7					1
		2		5				

Clue:

Psalm __ __ : __

O LORD, how great are thy works! and thy thoughts are very deep.

PUZZLE 27

		7			9			2
4		3						
	1		2	5	6			7
			9	2				
2	6						3	9
				7	1			
5			3	6	4		1	
						9		4
1			8			6		

Clue:

Psalm __ __ : __

Deliver me in thy righteousness, and cause me to escape: incline thine ear unto me, and save me.

PUZZLE 28

							3	
	2	1	3		7	9		
9				6		7	2	
	1	9	7	2		4		3
7		2		3	6	8	5	
	8	5		4				2
		3	6		8	5	9	
	9							

Clue:

2 Thessalonians __ : __ __

Comfort your hearts, and stablish you in every good word and work.

PUZZLE 29

Clue:

Ephesians __ : __ __

And be renewed in the spirit of your mind.

PUZZLE 30

Clue:

Matthew __ : __ __

And every one that heareth these sayings of mine, and doeth them not, shall be likened unto a foolish man, which built his house upon the sand.

PUZZLE 31

5	1	8						
4	9				2			
						4		8
	6			8	7			
2	3		9		4		8	6
			5	3			2	
1		2						
			7				3	2
						7	5	4

Clue:
Galatians __ : __ __

For in Christ Jesus neither circumcision availeth any thing, nor uncircumcision, but a new creature.

PUZZLE 32

					3	4		2
				6	7	1		
8							9	
7			3		2		1	5
		6				3		
1	8		6		9			4
	3							7
		9	7	4				
6			7	2				

Clue:
Psalm __ __ : __

My soul shall make her boast in the LORD: the humble shall hear thereof, and be glad.

PUZZLE 33

	1		2				9	
5				6		░░	░░	░░
		8	3	1		7	4	
		5	1					
	6	9				1	2	
					2	9		
	9	2		7	3	5		
			6				7	
	7				4		1	

Clue:

Jeremiah __ : __ __

O generation, see ye the word of the Lord.

PUZZLE 34

					4	5	3	
		7			2	4		9
5					9			2
			5			9		7
	8	3				2	5	
7		5			6			
3			6					1
6		8	2			7		
	7	4	8			░░	░░	░░

Clue:

Psalm __ __ : __

My soul, wait thou only upon God; for my expectation is from him.

PUZZLE 35

				6		7		2
							6	1
		6	4	1			3	
	2	1		5	9			
	5		7		6		8	
			1	4		6	2	
	1			7	4	3		
5	9							
4		3		9				

Clue:

Hebrews __ __ : __

Jesus Christ the same yesterday, and to day, and for ever.

PUZZLE 36

6	3			4		7		1
								8
			3		5		6	
	9		2	8				4
5				3	4		2	
	6		5		8			
1								
4		7		9			3	2

Clue:

Psalm __ __ : __

His glory is great in thy salvation: honour and majesty hast thou laid upon him.

PUZZLE 37

2	9							
6		1	2					
5	8			1		9		
				5			7	3
		5	3		4	6		
3	1			9				
		6		4			3	7
					6	8		9
							6	5

Clue:
Genesis __ __ : __
And I will make my covenant between me and thee, and will multiply thee exceedingly.

PUZZLE 38

		8				4	1	
7						2		8
6					5			
			5	8		3		
8			7		6			9
		7		9	1			
			1					6
3		5						1
	6	2				7		

Clue:
Ecclesiastes __ : __ __
Then said I, Wisdom is better than strength.

PUZZLE 39

Clue:

Psalm __ __ : __

For in the time of trouble he shall hide me in his pavilion: in the secret of his tabernacle shall he hide me; he shall set me up upon a rock.

PUZZLE 40

Clue:

Philippians __ : __ __

But my God shall supply all your need according to his riches in glory by Christ Jesus.

PUZZLE 41

		9			5		4	3
6						8		
			9	7	2	1		
			4				9	
		4	1		9	5		
	3				2			
	9	2	7	5				
		8						5
7	4		6			9		

Clue:

Psalm __ __ : __

For thou, LORD, hast made me glad through thy work: I will triumph in the works of thy hands.

PUZZLE 42

			1		2		3	9
1		4					5	7
			3					
7			2	8			9	
		9				8		
	4			7	3			2
				6				
4	6					7		5
9	2		8		4			

Clue:

Romans __ __ : __

For whether we live, we live unto the Lord; and whether we die, we die unto the Lord: whether we live therefore, or die, we are the Lord's.

PUZZLE 43

		4				7		
9			6					
6	1		3			4		2
		9			4	3		
8								7
		2	1			5		
7		5			6		3	8
▓	▓	▓			8			9
		8				2		

Clue:

Psalm __ __ : __

The LORD is my shepherd; I shall not want.

PUZZLE 44

	2	8	4					
▓	▓	▓				4		6
7							2	
2			6		8	3		9
3				4				8
8		6	9		2			5
	6							7
9		5						
					3	9	1	

Clue:

Galatians __ : __ __

For, brethren, ye have been called unto liberty; only use not liberty
for an occasion to the flesh, but by love serve one another.

PUZZLE 45

Clue:
Ephesians __ : __ __
For no man ever yet hated his own flesh; but nourisheth and cherisheth it, even as the Lord the church.

PUZZLE 46

Clue:
2 Corinthians __ : __ __
For all things are for your sakes, that the abundant grace might through the thanksgiving of many redound to the glory of God.

PUZZLE 47

	9		8	1				2
	2			6				
					7		9	
8	7		9				2	
9		1				3		4
	3				5		7	6
	8		7					
░	░	░		3			5	
7				9	6		4	

Clue:

Deuteronomy __ __ : __

And he hath brought us into this place, and hath given us this land, even a land that floweth with milk and honey.

PUZZLE 48

8					5	░	░	░
	1		2	4				
	2					1	6	
			8		9		4	6
		6		1		2		
4	8		3		7			
	3	9					7	
				8	2		5	
			7					4

Clue:

John __ : __ __

Come, see a man, which told me all things that ever I did: is not this the Christ?

PUZZLE 49

9				7			5	6
			1	4				2
		7				8	4	
	8	6		3	2			
			4	1		9	8	
	7	5				6		
6				9	7			
2	9			8				1

Clue:

Romans __ : __ __

Therefore we conclude that a man is justified by faith without the deeds of the law.

PUZZLE 50

				7		2		
7		2	3			8		1
			9			4		7
			7	3		6		4
4								3
1		3		2	6			
2		4			5			
5		9			7	1		2
		8		9				

Clue:

Matthew __ : __ __

And his disciples came to him, and awoke him, saying, Lord, save us: we perish.

ANSWERS TO SUDOKU PUZZLE CLUES

PUZZLE 1: 174

PUZZLE 2: 416

PUZZLE 3: 918

PUZZLE 4: 819

PUZZLE 5: 251

PUZZLE 6: 261

PUZZLE 7: 165

PUZZLE 8: 265

PUZZLE 9: 618

PUZZLE 10: 165

PUZZLE 11: 527

PUZZLE 12: 286

PUZZLE 13: 214

PUZZLE 14: 829

PUZZLE 15: 619

PUZZLE 16: 812

PUZZLE 17: 293

PUZZLE 18: 236

PUZZLE 19: 273

PUZZLE 20: 615

PUZZLE 21: 126

PUZZLE 22: 812

PUZZLE 23: 916

PUZZLE 24: 918

PUZZLE 25: 142

PUZZLE 26: 925

PUZZLE 27: 712

PUZZLE 28: 217

PUZZLE 29: 423

PUZZLE 30: 726

PUZZLE 31: 615

PUZZLE 32: 342

PUZZLE 33: 231

PUZZLE 34: 625

PUZZLE 35: 138

PUZZLE 36: 215

PUZZLE 37: 172

PUZZLE 38: 916

PUZZLE 39: 275

PUZZLE 40: 419

PUZZLE 41: 924

PUZZLE 42: 148

PUZZLE 43: 231

PUZZLE 44: 513

PUZZLE 45: 529

PUZZLE 46: 415

PUZZLE 47: 269

PUZZLE 48: 429

PUZZLE 49: 328

PUZZLE 50: 825

SUDOKU PUZZLE SOLUTIONS

PUZZLE 1

1	7	4	6	9	5	2	8	3
8	5	3	1	2	4	6	9	7
2	9	6	7	8	3	5	1	4
3	1	5	9	6	7	8	4	2
4	6	9	2	3	8	7	5	1
7	2	8	5	4	1	3	6	9
5	8	1	4	7	2	9	3	6
6	4	7	3	5	9	1	2	8
9	3	2	8	1	6	4	7	5

PUZZLE 3

2	9	8	5	7	1	3	6	4
1	5	4	6	9	3	2	7	8
3	7	6	4	8	2	9	1	5
4	8	7	3	6	5	1	9	2
6	2	3	9	1	8	4	5	7
9	1	5	7	2	4	8	3	6
7	6	2	1	4	9	5	8	3
8	3	1	2	5	7	6	4	9
5	4	9	8	3	6	7	2	1

PUZZLE 2

7	2	4	3	8	9	1	6	5
5	9	6	4	1	7	3	8	2
8	3	1	2	6	5	9	7	4
9	6	7	5	4	1	2	3	8
2	8	5	7	9	3	4	1	6
1	4	3	6	2	8	5	9	7
6	1	9	8	5	2	7	4	3
4	7	2	1	3	6	8	5	9
3	5	8	9	7	4	6	2	1

PUZZLE 4

8	7	1	9	4	3	5	6	2
4	5	9	7	6	2	1	8	3
2	6	3	1	5	8	7	4	9
9	8	5	4	3	6	2	1	7
3	2	7	8	1	9	4	5	6
6	1	4	5	2	7	3	9	8
1	3	6	2	8	4	9	7	5
7	4	2	6	9	5	8	3	1
5	9	8	3	7	1	6	2	4

PUZZLE 5

3	4	5	6	9	8	2	1	7
9	1	7	4	2	3	8	5	6
6	2	8	7	5	1	4	3	9
8	6	9	2	1	4	3	7	5
1	3	2	5	8	7	9	6	4
5	7	4	9	3	6	1	2	8
4	8	3	1	6	5	7	9	2
7	9	6	3	4	2	5	8	1
2	5	1	8	7	9	6	4	3

PUZZLE 7

6	2	3	8	9	1	5	4	7
5	1	8	3	4	7	9	6	2
4	9	7	5	2	6	8	1	3
7	4	6	2	1	8	3	9	5
3	5	1	6	7	9	2	8	4
9	8	2	4	5	3	1	7	6
1	6	9	7	3	2	4	5	8
8	3	4	1	6	5	7	2	9
2	7	5	9	8	4	6	3	1

PUZZLE 6

4	1	8	7	2	9	3	6	5
5	2	6	4	8	3	7	1	9
3	9	7	1	5	6	4	2	8
7	5	9	6	3	8	1	4	2
6	4	3	9	1	2	8	5	7
1	8	2	5	7	4	9	3	6
8	3	4	2	9	5	6	7	1
9	7	5	3	6	1	2	8	4
2	6	1	8	4	7	5	9	3

PUZZLE 8

3	1	7	9	4	2	6	8	5
2	9	6	5	1	8	3	7	4
5	4	8	6	7	3	9	2	1
8	7	3	4	5	6	1	9	2
4	5	9	1	2	7	8	6	3
1	6	2	8	3	9	4	5	7
9	3	4	2	6	5	7	1	8
7	8	5	3	9	1	2	4	6
6	2	1	7	8	4	5	3	9

PUZZLE 9

5	7	9	2	8	1	4	6	3
3	8	1	4	6	5	9	2	7
2	4	6	9	7	3	8	5	1
4	2	5	7	3	6	1	9	8
6	1	7	8	2	9	5	3	4
8	9	3	1	5	4	2	7	6
9	3	8	5	4	7	6	1	2
7	5	2	6	1	8	3	4	9
1	6	4	3	9	2	7	8	5

PUZZLE 11

5	2	3	7	4	9	8	6	1
8	6	1	2	5	3	9	7	4
9	4	7	8	6	1	2	5	3
2	7	8	9	3	4	6	1	5
6	1	9	5	2	7	4	3	8
4	3	5	6	1	8	7	2	9
7	5	4	1	9	6	3	8	2
3	8	2	4	7	5	1	9	6
1	9	6	3	8	2	5	4	7

PUZZLE 10

6	5	8	3	9	7	2	1	4
3	7	9	4	2	1	6	5	8
2	1	4	8	5	6	3	9	7
8	9	3	2	1	4	7	6	5
1	6	5	7	3	9	4	8	2
7	4	2	6	8	5	1	3	9
9	3	6	5	4	2	8	7	1
5	2	7	1	6	8	9	4	3
4	8	1	9	7	3	5	2	6

PUZZLE 12

8	5	9	7	6	4	3	2	1
1	3	2	5	9	8	7	6	4
4	6	7	1	2	3	9	5	8
2	8	5	9	4	7	6	1	3
3	7	1	2	8	6	4	9	5
6	9	4	3	5	1	8	7	2
5	2	8	4	7	9	1	3	6
9	4	3	6	1	2	5	8	7
7	1	6	8	3	5	2	4	9

PUZZLE 13

1	6	5	3	7	8	2	4	9
4	2	7	5	9	6	3	8	1
3	9	8	4	2	1	7	5	6
2	1	4	8	3	9	5	6	7
6	7	3	1	4	5	9	2	8
5	8	9	2	6	7	4	1	3
7	3	2	6	1	4	8	9	5
8	4	1	9	5	3	6	7	2
9	5	6	7	8	2	1	3	4

PUZZLE 15

5	8	6	2	1	4	3	7	9
1	4	3	9	5	7	2	8	6
2	9	7	6	8	3	4	1	5
3	2	5	8	7	6	9	4	1
8	7	4	1	3	9	6	5	2
6	1	9	5	4	2	7	3	8
9	3	1	4	6	5	8	2	7
4	5	2	7	9	8	1	6	3
7	6	8	3	2	1	5	9	4

PUZZLE 14

9	7	8	1	4	2	3	5	6
2	6	3	7	9	5	8	4	1
5	1	4	6	8	3	9	2	7
7	5	1	8	2	9	4	6	3
3	4	2	5	6	7	1	9	8
6	8	9	3	1	4	2	7	5
1	9	5	4	3	6	7	8	2
8	2	6	9	7	1	5	3	4
4	3	7	2	5	8	6	1	9

PUZZLE 16

6	9	5	8	7	4	1	2	3
3	8	1	2	6	5	7	9	4
2	4	7	9	1	3	6	8	5
1	2	8	5	9	6	3	4	7
9	6	3	4	8	7	2	5	1
5	7	4	1	3	2	9	6	8
7	3	9	6	4	8	5	1	2
4	5	6	7	2	1	8	3	9
8	1	2	3	5	9	4	7	6

PUZZLE 17

9	1	4	2	6	5	7	3	8
7	3	8	4	1	9	6	2	5
6	5	2	7	8	3	4	9	1
2	9	3	5	4	7	1	8	6
5	7	1	8	2	6	9	4	3
8	4	6	3	9	1	2	5	7
1	6	5	9	3	4	8	7	2
3	8	9	1	7	2	5	6	4
4	2	7	6	5	8	3	1	9

PUZZLE 19

1	4	5	9	8	7	6	3	2
8	3	6	4	2	1	9	5	7
7	2	9	3	6	5	4	8	1
2	9	4	8	7	6	3	1	5
5	6	7	1	9	3	8	2	4
3	8	1	5	4	2	7	6	9
4	1	8	6	5	9	2	7	3
6	7	3	2	1	4	5	9	8
9	5	2	7	3	8	1	4	6

PUZZLE 18

9	1	4	6	2	3	5	7	8
5	6	7	8	9	4	1	2	3
3	8	2	1	5	7	6	4	9
4	3	6	9	8	1	2	5	7
7	5	1	3	6	2	9	8	4
2	9	8	7	4	5	3	1	6
1	2	3	4	7	9	8	6	5
8	7	5	2	3	6	4	9	1
6	4	9	5	1	8	7	3	2

PUZZLE 20

7	3	8	4	5	6	2	9	1
4	6	9	7	2	1	8	5	3
1	5	2	9	3	8	6	7	4
3	8	1	2	4	9	5	6	7
5	9	6	1	7	3	4	8	2
2	7	4	6	8	5	3	1	9
6	1	5	3	9	2	7	4	8
9	4	3	8	6	7	1	2	5
8	2	7	5	1	4	9	3	6

PUZZLE 21

9	3	6	8	5	7	2	4	1
4	8	2	6	1	3	7	9	5
7	5	1	2	9	4	6	3	8
5	2	7	3	4	8	9	1	6
6	1	4	5	7	9	3	8	2
3	9	8	1	2	6	4	5	7
2	4	9	7	8	1	5	6	3
1	7	3	4	6	5	8	2	9
8	6	5	9	3	2	1	7	4

PUZZLE 23

3	5	4	7	2	8	1	6	9
7	9	8	6	4	1	2	3	5
1	6	2	5	9	3	7	4	8
5	8	9	4	6	2	3	7	1
2	7	3	9	1	5	4	8	6
6	4	1	3	8	7	5	9	2
9	1	6	2	3	4	8	5	7
4	2	7	8	5	9	6	1	3
8	3	5	1	7	6	9	2	4

PUZZLE 22

7	9	3	2	4	1	5	6	8
5	6	4	3	7	8	2	9	1
8	1	2	6	5	9	3	7	4
9	7	5	4	1	3	8	2	6
4	2	8	7	6	5	1	3	9
6	3	1	9	8	2	4	5	7
2	5	6	1	9	4	7	8	3
1	8	9	5	3	7	6	4	2
3	4	7	8	2	6	9	1	5

PUZZLE 24

2	1	9	7	5	8	3	6	4
5	7	6	2	4	3	9	1	8
3	8	4	9	1	6	5	7	2
1	3	5	8	7	2	6	4	9
6	9	8	5	3	4	7	2	1
7	4	2	6	9	1	8	5	3
9	5	1	4	8	7	2	3	6
8	6	3	1	2	5	4	9	7
4	2	7	3	6	9	1	8	5

PUZZLE 25

7	8	9	3	5	6	1	4	2
6	2	5	4	1	9	3	7	8
4	1	3	7	2	8	6	5	9
1	5	8	9	7	3	2	6	4
3	6	4	2	8	5	7	9	1
2	9	7	1	6	4	8	3	5
9	7	1	6	4	2	5	8	3
8	4	2	5	3	7	9	1	6
5	3	6	8	9	1	4	2	7

PUZZLE 27

6	5	7	4	3	9	1	8	2
4	2	3	1	8	7	5	9	6
9	1	8	2	5	6	3	4	7
7	8	5	9	2	3	4	6	1
2	6	1	5	4	8	7	3	9
3	9	4	6	7	1	8	2	5
5	7	9	3	6	4	2	1	8
8	3	6	7	1	2	9	5	4
1	4	2	8	9	5	6	7	3

PUZZLE 26

9	7	5	2	4	8	1	3	6
4	1	6	5	9	3	7	8	2
3	2	8	1	7	6	5	4	9
8	5	1	6	3	7	9	2	4
7	6	4	9	2	5	8	1	3
2	3	9	4	8	1	6	7	5
6	9	7	3	1	4	2	5	8
5	8	3	7	6	2	4	9	1
1	4	2	8	5	9	3	6	7

PUZZLE 28

4	6	7	2	5	9	1	3	8
5	2	1	3	8	7	9	4	6
9	3	8	4	6	1	7	2	5
8	1	9	7	2	5	4	6	3
3	5	6	8	9	4	2	1	7
7	4	2	1	3	6	8	5	9
1	8	5	9	4	3	6	7	2
2	7	3	6	1	8	5	9	4
6	9	4	5	7	2	3	8	1

PUZZLE 29

6	4	8	3	7	9	2	1	5
3	1	9	2	6	5	7	4	8
7	2	5	1	8	4	3	6	9
1	6	3	9	5	2	4	8	7
8	9	4	7	3	6	1	5	2
2	5	7	8	4	1	6	9	3
4	3	1	5	9	7	8	2	6
9	7	2	6	1	8	5	3	4
5	8	6	4	2	3	9	7	1

PUZZLE 31

5	1	8	4	6	9	2	7	3
4	9	3	8	7	2	6	1	5
7	2	6	1	5	3	4	9	8
9	6	5	2	8	7	3	4	1
2	3	7	9	1	4	5	8	6
8	4	1	5	3	6	9	2	7
1	7	2	3	4	5	8	6	9
6	5	4	7	9	8	1	3	2
3	8	9	6	2	1	7	5	4

PUZZLE 30

8	9	5	3	4	1	7	2	6
6	7	3	9	2	5	1	8	4
4	2	1	8	7	6	3	5	9
7	6	8	1	9	2	4	3	5
3	4	9	5	6	8	2	7	1
5	1	2	4	3	7	6	9	8
9	3	6	2	8	4	5	1	7
2	5	4	7	1	9	8	6	3
1	8	7	6	5	3	9	4	2

PUZZLE 32

9	7	5	8	1	3	4	6	2
3	4	2	9	6	7	1	5	8
8	6	1	5	2	4	7	9	3
7	9	4	3	8	2	6	1	5
5	2	6	4	7	1	3	8	9
1	8	3	6	5	9	2	7	4
4	3	8	1	9	6	5	2	7
2	1	9	7	4	5	8	3	6
6	5	7	2	3	8	9	4	1

PUZZLE 33

3	1	7	2	4	5	6	9	8
9	5	4	7	8	6	2	3	1
6	2	8	3	1	9	7	4	5
2	3	5	1	9	7	4	8	6
4	6	9	5	3	8	1	2	7
7	8	1	4	6	2	9	5	3
1	9	2	8	7	3	5	6	4
5	4	3	6	2	1	8	7	9
8	7	6	9	5	4	3	1	2

PUZZLE 35

1	3	8	9	6	5	7	4	2
2	4	5	3	8	7	9	6	1
9	7	6	4	1	2	5	3	8
6	2	1	8	5	9	4	7	3
3	5	4	7	2	6	1	8	9
7	8	9	1	4	3	6	2	5
8	1	2	5	7	4	3	9	6
5	9	7	6	3	8	2	1	4
4	6	3	2	9	1	8	5	7

PUZZLE 34

2	9	1	7	6	4	5	3	8
8	3	7	1	5	2	4	6	9
5	4	6	3	8	9	1	7	2
4	6	2	5	3	8	9	1	7
9	8	3	4	1	7	2	5	6
7	1	5	9	2	6	3	8	4
3	2	9	6	7	5	8	4	1
6	5	8	2	4	1	7	9	3
1	7	4	8	9	3	6	2	5

PUZZLE 36

6	3	9	8	4	2	7	5	1
2	1	5	9	6	7	3	4	8
8	7	4	3	1	5	2	6	9
3	9	6	2	8	1	5	7	4
7	4	2	6	5	9	1	8	3
5	8	1	7	3	4	9	2	6
9	6	3	5	2	8	4	1	7
1	2	8	4	7	3	6	9	5
4	5	7	1	9	6	8	3	2

PUZZLE 37

2	9	3	8	6	5	7	1	4
6	4	1	2	7	9	3	5	8
5	8	7	4	1	3	9	2	6
9	6	8	1	5	2	4	7	3
7	2	5	3	8	4	6	9	1
3	1	4	6	9	7	5	8	2
8	5	6	9	4	1	2	3	7
1	7	2	5	3	6	8	4	9
4	3	9	7	2	8	1	6	5

PUZZLE 39

9	7	6	2	8	5	1	4	3
8	4	3	9	1	6	2	7	5
1	5	2	3	7	4	9	8	6
4	9	8	7	5	1	6	3	2
6	3	5	8	4	2	7	9	1
7	2	1	6	3	9	8	5	4
2	8	9	4	6	3	5	1	7
3	1	7	5	2	8	4	6	9
5	6	4	1	9	7	3	2	8

PUZZLE 38

2	9	8	3	6	7	4	1	5
7	5	3	4	1	9	2	6	8
6	4	1	8	2	5	9	3	7
9	1	6	5	8	4	3	7	2
8	2	4	7	3	6	1	5	9
5	3	7	2	9	1	6	8	4
4	8	9	1	7	3	5	2	6
3	7	5	6	4	2	8	9	1
1	6	2	9	5	8	7	4	3

PUZZLE 40

7	4	1	2	6	9	8	5	3
6	9	8	5	3	4	7	2	1
5	2	3	7	1	8	9	6	4
2	8	5	4	7	1	6	3	9
4	1	9	6	5	3	2	7	8
3	7	6	9	8	2	4	1	5
9	6	7	3	4	5	1	8	2
1	5	4	8	2	7	3	9	6
8	3	2	1	9	6	5	4	7

PUZZLE 41

8	1	9	2	6	5	7	4	3
6	2	7	3	4	1	8	5	9
4	5	3	8	9	7	2	1	6
5	7	1	4	8	6	3	9	2
2	8	4	1	3	9	5	6	7
9	3	6	5	7	2	4	8	1
1	9	2	7	5	8	6	3	4
3	6	8	9	2	4	1	7	5
7	4	5	6	1	3	9	2	8

PUZZLE 43

5	8	4	2	9	1	7	6	3
9	2	3	6	4	7	8	5	1
6	1	7	3	8	5	4	9	2
1	5	9	8	7	4	3	2	6
8	4	6	5	3	2	9	1	7
3	7	2	1	6	9	5	8	4
7	9	5	4	2	6	1	3	8
2	3	1	7	5	8	6	4	9
4	6	8	9	1	3	2	7	5

PUZZLE 42

5	7	8	1	4	2	6	3	9
1	3	4	6	9	8	2	5	7
6	9	2	5	3	7	1	4	8
7	1	3	2	8	5	4	9	6
2	5	9	4	1	6	8	7	3
8	4	6	9	7	3	5	1	2
3	8	5	7	6	1	9	2	4
4	6	1	3	2	9	7	8	5
9	2	7	8	5	4	3	6	1

PUZZLE 44

6	2	8	4	1	9	7	5	3
5	1	3	2	8	7	4	9	6
7	9	4	3	5	6	8	2	1
2	5	1	6	7	8	3	4	9
3	7	9	1	4	5	2	6	8
8	4	6	9	3	2	1	7	5
1	6	2	8	9	4	5	3	7
9	3	5	7	2	1	6	8	4
4	8	7	5	6	3	9	1	2

PUZZLE 45

9	7	8	2	4	6	3	1	5
3	4	1	8	5	9	7	6	2
2	5	6	1	3	7	4	9	8
6	3	5	4	8	2	1	7	9
4	1	7	9	6	5	2	8	3
8	9	2	3	7	1	5	4	6
5	2	9	6	1	4	8	3	7
7	8	4	5	9	3	6	2	1
1	6	3	7	2	8	9	5	4

PUZZLE 47

6	9	7	8	1	4	5	3	2
5	2	8	3	6	9	4	1	7
1	4	3	5	2	7	6	9	8
8	7	6	9	4	3	1	2	5
9	5	1	6	7	2	3	8	4
4	3	2	1	8	5	9	7	6
3	8	4	7	5	1	2	6	9
2	6	9	4	3	8	7	5	1
7	1	5	2	9	6	8	4	3

PUZZLE 46

5	2	4	8	1	7	6	3	9
6	8	7	4	9	3	2	1	5
1	9	3	6	5	2	4	7	8
9	3	2	5	7	6	1	8	4
4	1	5	3	2	8	7	9	6
8	7	6	1	4	9	3	5	2
2	6	8	7	3	5	9	4	1
3	4	9	2	8	1	5	6	7
7	5	1	9	6	4	8	2	3

PUZZLE 48

8	6	3	1	7	5	4	2	9
9	1	5	2	4	6	7	3	8
7	2	4	9	3	8	1	6	5
5	7	1	8	2	9	3	4	6
3	9	6	5	1	4	2	8	7
4	8	2	3	6	7	5	9	1
6	3	9	4	5	1	8	7	2
1	4	7	6	8	2	9	5	3
2	5	8	7	9	3	6	1	4

PUZZLE 49

9	2	4	8	7	3	1	5	6
5	6	8	1	4	9	7	3	2
1	3	7	2	6	5	8	4	9
7	8	6	9	3	2	4	1	5
4	1	9	7	5	8	2	6	3
3	5	2	4	1	6	9	8	7
8	7	5	3	2	1	6	9	4
6	4	1	5	9	7	3	2	8
2	9	3	6	8	4	5	7	1

PUZZLE 50

9	4	1	5	7	8	2	3	6
7	5	2	3	6	4	8	9	1
3	8	6	9	1	2	4	5	7
8	2	5	7	3	9	6	1	4
4	6	7	8	5	1	9	2	3
1	9	3	4	2	6	5	7	8
2	7	4	1	8	5	3	6	9
5	3	9	6	4	7	1	8	2
6	1	8	2	9	3	7	4	5

Part Four
WORD SEARCH

PUZZLE 1: LESSONS

```
M D O O F S X X K F X Y A R A X Y D A S R
M R M K N O X Y B E M L I I R H L S E X K
K D U Z M X R Q R V C A C J O P F L C R V
G T R B T T G G E R Z Y B U B X T O R J R
D S E H T I T K I F H A J K A C S R O P L
A A K V O V C U B V U R J Z L J E H V E B
R D G O O E I J W A E T Z T M W V O I Z L
K U X X G L I E O H D E A S A C R R D J E
N L U V J H Q G T T Y B P R L V A V E Y S
E T V T J U S T I C E R D P L W H C T U S
S E A Y E C P L X V Z A L E P S E I I A I
S R N S S I M K N I I E E W H V R Q X Y N
B Y W I G A R B F S O N D D W A U M A W G
S W L P A N T O X V H L G I H G K W V J S
F S H T N O I S R E V N O C N S W C R U Q
E T B G V C S Y O E N B R W Y O J S X M F
S J Y I G B X V U P B E G U R F N O V H X
W E Y T B W Z Z N M A N M R C Z N S Y A A
E S N Z D Q Q S P G Q K A I U N L V R T I
R E S U R R E C T I O N M I E M G I M P J
D M L K T T O H J V G O X J S S P P G K A
```

ADULTERY	FORGIVE
APOSTASY	GIVING
BETRAYAL	HARVEST
BLESSINGS	JUSTICE
CHARITY	LABOR
CONVERSION	LOVE
DARKNESS	NARROWWAY
DIVORCE	RESURRECTION
ENEMIES	REWARD
FOOD	TITHES

PUZZLE 2: ABRAHAM'S PROGENY

```
H P S F D F A D B S V B S V M R D F Z N V
E D X Y E R O Z Z L E A M H S I V V H A M
K F W L E H K H O O V F G C G Q H U E D P
I M R A C B A Z U A Y M I G C J E H I E P
Y C F O I M W G Z Z V F N H I G C M R D V
H U N R M J J N I Y V B I T W G I E U V L
J A P A M I R U H S S A I O G D Z L F Y A
H B H D X M X T D A U H M J I R N N L E E
S S S H Y M A P W O S X U A R S W I P D G
O L A T E H I Z G Y Q X N B C U T M G J O
S O V Q A Z B Q Q T H R T E F E C O O K E
U L B N D Y R B A N F I M N K U U K R L M
N I F D B A R O N T L E I W F T S A A E E
A A C W J I J J N H Y J A P H H H J D U A
J N R O I C N P S W Q O R Z A R V T E M B
E T J M L C J L P M S X H N X W R N K M B
F R K B I I Y Q R S M V P X Q H A Z Z I M
N Z D U E Z N W H H A L E H S P G R M M Y
E G P U N D O E R Z R O I B G R X K K X E L
U W V U Z P B W X S O Y G I I O Y W Z Y T
B V H V D A Q R E S H U A H X M G B U L L
```

ASSHURIM	MIDIAN
CARMI	MIZZAH
DEDAN	NAHATH
EPHRAIM	NEBAJOTH
HANOCH	PEREZ
HEZRON	SHAMMAH
ISHMAEL	SHEBA
JOKSHAN	SHELAH
KEDAR	SHUAH
LEUMMIM	ZIMRAN

PUZZLE 3: PRISONERS AND CAPTIVES

```
T F K M F K F J X M O W E H Y H Z E N E K
Y U I I U Y N B U Q B S P N P X N S H S C
Z B H M A Z A R I A H K V K F Z B Y O T D
W B A O Z C K O Q X V Z Z D G V Z J J H H
N O A H Y E E F Y A K V V V Z V T V V E W
L T F Z M D D D J V Z P F G H S A Y T R Z
J J P T T M R E R U U K S I M Y T U N V D
O C E L R I E U K O W R W V F C H J W X P
B R T E I U T H M I M I Y J L Q G Z G R I
N J E I B G L X H D A Y H E S S A N A M L
B Z R A A M I A H L O H Z W P H J R E B O
Z J J O S E S N G E E Y E N E H P E T S S
Y D I F L I Z O U J C X L J I S W L D J R
I K Z U M S L Y D F D Y E Q A A D J P H Q
M G D R D O M A I X H K I W P C C K P D N
A A K Y E R N W S A F J N P M U O E M T S
X D T E P F G E I Q V M A A U V S B Q L P
R W A A T J X A Q V O G D U H O Q V I K U
Y V K E K S S I H A X J I L J F J D E X U
N L H A P I A V O W T L G B Y H A G A R L
Y M G B U R P W N R U B O R K R X O W I I
```

AZARIAH	MANASSEH
BIGVAI	MORDECAI
CAIN	NOAH
DANIEL	PAUL
ESTHER	PETER
HAGAR	RAAMIAH
ISAIAH	SILAS
JACOB	STEPHEN
JOHN	ZEDEKIAH
JOSEPH	

PUZZLE 4: DANIEL

```
L  L  H  F  V  C  Y  P  B  Q  N  M  B  P  I  H  S  R  O  W  W
O  Y  B  E  U  D  D  Y  I  E  R  U  T  A  R  E  T  I  L  O  V
D  B  F  V  A  R  G  I  F  T  E  D  H  H  B  L  X  W  U  Q  K
I  R  Y  N  Q  X  N  X  M  N  X  J  B  N  X  Y  C  N  P  A  M
R  Z  I  D  Q  B  W  A  C  W  S  X  R  B  N  S  L  R  L  W  Q
R  E  N  N  G  P  R  A  C  K  M  E  U  Z  N  A  O  O  N  V  L
L  R  T  O  F  G  O  H  K  E  Y  V  R  D  G  C  J  B  N  G  W
U  X  E  N  B  L  S  P  X  P  B  I  G  C  L  B  F  F  Y  F  C
O  J  R  Y  S  J  B  E  L  T  E  S  H  A  Z  Z  A  R  G  G  M
A  P  P  T  E  H  U  S  I  S  L  A  M  N  Q  P  H  K  K  D  D
L  B  R  O  I  T  H  D  N  T  L  A  S  Y  E  U  A  V  O  O  R
I  P  E  I  T  A  S  O  F  D  T  K  Y  C  Z  M  H  W  G  N  M
O  T  T  D  D  J  N  L  E  I  N  N  W  N  P  L  R  F  U  O  U
N  N  I  R  N  A  C  A  O  Z  W  L  O  J  M  D  O  U  F  N  I
S  F  A  L  P  E  N  N  H  Q  B  P  V  Y  G  N  P  E  O  D  R
C  C  Z  Z  C  S  G  M  V  Y  K  Y  W  K  O  N  Q  F  W  F  U
H  A  Y  A  X  F  R  O  Q  H  P  T  P  S  L  D  G  D  N  D  Y
B  H  W  S  B  F  B  G  M  M  N  N  X  C  M  T  R  X  B  D  Z
J  T  I  R  F  T  E  J  S  V  H  Q  R  X  O  G  I  E  I  T  G
D  P  G  O  O  D  L  O  O  K  I  N  G  F  L  A  Z  E  A  H  E
B  Z  D  U  C  F  U  U  N  D  E  R  S  T  A  N  D  O  I  M  G
```

ABEDNEGO	IDOL
BABYLON	INTERPRET
BELTESHAZZAR	LIONS
CHALDEANS	LITERATURE
DANIEL	PROCLAMATION
DREAM	SHADRACH
FOUR MEN	SON OF GOD
FURNACE	UNDERSTAND
GIFTED	WORSHIP
GOOD LOOKING	

PUZZLE 5: THE TABERNACLE

```
Z M R P T J J E S D F C I L Q B V B B O F
Y R A U T C N A S E H S L N V Z F Z G Q L
L K J M B J P Q M R I Y H S T I B U C I Z
R S Q J B G P Q Q A W L H O A S C G S N Z
G F T A J D D O G T C J O W W R N Q I C N
G D R K X X L Z Q O Z K D H Q B S Q U E E
N N U B R Y U D V N I A L A F S R H F N L
L A O E M Q N E O E E U F I J O T E F S C
I T C L U F N O J M Z U Z C L C Y I A E A
X S R L U A Q S U E R H T A K G W L P D N
U P E O N B A J G N F J L C R D B O O R R
Z M N T T X K Q I T R W Z A J H K V S H E
Q A N D L S U S D K Z X F V X M T U V V B
W L I S J C H Z D E T C E R E W N S I U A
Z H B S R I V J L C N G U R O F U H Y A T
Q S V S N O N Z P N X M C E R D S V H F I
S E G G G L L O Q B X Y K P E V S F D F J
X I S L A N X O G Y S N K B V X L G W A Y
N F H Z Y L M R C E U R S W A R I V E Q E
D M M N N X L D A Z H Y G J L N Y F L Q Y
Q J F G F G J T S I K M N V S M R O L E D
```

ACACIA	INCENSE
ATONEMENT	INNERCOURT
COLORS	LAMPSTAND
COVENANT	LAVER
CUBITS	MERCYSEAT
DWELL	ONYX
ERECTED	SANCTUARY
FURNISHINGS	SHOWBREAD
HOLY OF HOLIES	TABERNACLE

PUZZLE 6: DREAMERS

```
K U V K U P X J E M Z Z J G O V C L T J J
H T T D X W L Z U L H O H A A G C D X K Y
R E T E P S O L O M O N O A F D H L V E G
Z R D J P H T Q S N M X B I I H A L B Y N
X H U N N U A M E R J A N T M M E B P S T
I Q L L X T A O H N K U A T L B E V Q A D
Z F U Y E T N Q R E B A H C E I T R L S M
G J N C T I A J R A J Q X P S V D K E L H
H F V D O P N K J D H H P K D L O V J J U
A N M C E A I A Z P K P A W B X S O K N R
I H A B A B A T D L H N U B N E S L H E L
R E H M L I S E M E Q L L E M E X O R W B
A X A T R M Z I O C A H Z A P P J A N A V
H K R V B E V P D W O A J H F L E Z A U A
C M B S U L N O T O D I Q C Y B P L A U M
E L A A U E C X T F X A D N P G A E Y H Y
Z H E L B C F Q F L O S Y U J M S G V R S
E K U O G H O Q C W E I C W A T U G A B H
Z A C M J T Y N W R E P P Q T D O M F B W
P A G E D H M D O T H T R Q I N K Y N O G
J N D Y Z Y R J Z Z A E Z O Y B P I V D Q
```

ABIMELECH	JEREMIAH
ABRAHAM	JOHN
ANANIAS	JOSEPH
BAKER	MARY
BAALAM	PAUL
CUPBEARER	PETER
DANIEL	PHAROAH
ISAIAH	SALOME
JACOB	SOLOMON
JAMES	ZECHARIAH

PUZZLE 7: KIN TO KING SAUL

```
K P H F W A L I X N C J S J W X W H E N C
F Z H W H S H E A R I A H Z O I G P N M S
M X Z I L Z R Y F G V S O U L H R V K W M
T B O W D J K R K R I K F F N Y S M Q D A
Q O W D G E J D E O K W D M Y N D I I S L
G C N J E V S P Z B X S D E A D B B E T C
K H M N C R H O R A R W M I H D G K I A H
U E I V W A G J P D W R V K P W I Q Y H I
V R B Q I E J N U I V B N K X S T W Z R S
P U C A D F X S A A K F Z B H V Y D F E H
B S H O M A N V L H V P B H Y G E L J A U
J G R R B P M L A A B B I R E M L L G R A
F O F P W P U K P A K J I S H M A E L O B
K L F N Y R H N J Y Z B C Z Q J I D Q E K
M V N V Z V U Q O P J M H Y F J Z L S T R
W J J E B G M C N A B T A I W G F G N F N
H L W Z N H T S R S R T S V Q B Q N A V Y
M B Q Y S A Q A S G T T A Q E A A M D G F
Y C M D M E H K L S A V E F V T K A A E C
U Z J C I E C J I S H K L D W X H G D U G
V H Q T R B K F C P H Z E U B B I N E A O
```

AHIO	KISH
AZMAVETH	MALCHISHUA
BINEA	MERIBBAAL
BOCHERU	NADAD
ELEASAH	OBADIAH
GEDOR	REPHAIAH
HANEN	SHEARIAH
ISHMAEL	TAHREA
JARAH	TIMRI

PUZZLE 8: JUDAH'S OFFSPRING

```
O S L O G A L A S G I B J E X P Q V D B K
J F B H A B T R M H E B S G A K L V H F M
R H B D Z M S F O U H J E G E C D E I M T
C O G O E K A H X I O D P V L D A J B U B
Z Z X W Z D N M M R S H H O O H V Q D L K
I A Y J C J O S K U J Q A R V Y X H N L S
N A O F F B N O E T L M H U I Y P Y S A A
L O M Y Z C A G O P M A V E P N M E T H M
E R R A S M N Z N S F P A X I P G M A S E
L Q U B S K C Y R H R Z M R F F A S M G H
D G K T E I P N T N A N A J R H A T Q L S
N F A M E H S A C A D H H E A E Q A H E E
W U X A K L Z D Y T X M S R L H J S C V A
D K B O E O A R X H Y R I E Z A D L I Q V
O A E N I I T P R A Y B L Q R K V A A S U
U R B Y L A S W X N Z B E H Q A I K I B A
U Z Y A Y T G M U U K U D T A L M L W Y S
M V F G Z T C K C Q U Z A E H R M I O G V
J L Z M U A T A E C W H C A R Z A J J O D
O G O L B J U Y O N D U F M L G U N B R G
R C C U N U X Z Z Y S I I U O A J R I R H
```

ATTAI	MAON
BETHZUR	MARESHAH
ELEASAH	NATHAN
ELISHAMA	PALET
EPHAH	RAHAM
GAZEZ	SHALLUM
HARAN	SHEMA
HEBRON	SISAMAI
JAHDAI	TAPPUAH
JORKOAM	ZABAD

PUZZLE 9: KINGS BEFORE ISRAEL

```
Y V S J T T F L M T T W Q D Q P S C I E Y
C R W N A M J C Y W H W P C A E A H B M S
Z W P F B N T M E L W E M V P R G V Q B P
N V F A A O N Q E E B S L U N E A L V A C
V G L Q A J E C B H K E D E Z I H C L E M
D A W A F E N P M P P F R H U S H A M N S
K H G V P H A R O A H X A H S R I B Y K N
I C V N H B L Q B R H K X K S M A X H U M
S E V T B A I K T M J E U B D R X M I B O
J L S B T A V Q Y A W H C F I W M H A C C
K E C W S L B L D A J F A O Z L H B A H W
M M P B H H S P A C A E C X L F O C E U A
I I D U N A T W D Z P H J N U J P D A X L
T B T P Z N B I A S H U A V V C O P R M E
E A L D B A N I H S I U B P M R D X H E B
G Q I N D N N T K W A I I I L B K N Z K U
S T D S J F O F D D J M N A M F B V K E O
F E X L F U T V D B X G O H A Q G Q T R N
I T Y A A U E R T U Q M X Q R V V I J Y S
U M O M M N P R P S E M Z R I G F B K Z T
X H O H A M R M G R E A G Q P X Q A V V A
```

ABIMELECH   HOHAM
AMRAPHEL   HUSHAM
ARAD   JABIN
ARIOCH   JAPHIA
BAALHANAN   JOBAB
BALAK   MELCHIZEDEK
BELA   PHAROAH
BIRSHA   PIRAM
CHEDORLAOMER   REKEM
HADAD   SHINAB

PUZZLE 10: ALTARS

```
K W H E A V E N V Z W T E R F B S Y W Y F
L Q P A D Y S U K R D F J E S Z L Z E N E
E N V Z M S G D R S A L E M R A C S Y S O
G E D A M A S C U S T V X P C X F Y Z V I
I Y C P N J R R H H R K L A S N T O Q B W
B T F J I O Z B U E J A N H A R H P O B W
E S U E X C R P F M P A F X B D F Z E D N
O A O I B O L B O V A Z D R S S N E H T A
N C I H X A M B E N P K I T K E R Z B O H
P Z L T V D L H R H E R O M D S L E R A V
F A A I R B K W E Q K Z K Z H L T J R I B
M P E R T E W I P H F C J E M H E C K R Z
J S D B A D D R H A S V B L E K G I C A I
D Q F R M R W H I I J A A L M U S Z F M K
H L I T G L A G D R V L O O U X Q T E A U
M T G O B Y F T I O I L F Q Y M W Q Y S T
Q K O J Z I Y H M M E E H L X H C S O K K
S H E C H E M C L H D K D H G Q N S D J K
C M E E Q Z Z B N S N Q H W I L R X U O Y
C P B J I X F W L C Z I V S Q T G F N I C
F F M W D Q Z Z J X A U K W E R M A M L U
```

ARARAT

ATHENS

BEERSHEBA

BETHEL

CANAAN

CARMEL

DAMASCUS

EBAL

FIELD

GIBEON

HEAVEN

HEBRON

MAMRE

MIZPEH

MOREH

MORIAH

OPHRAH

RAMAH

REPHIDIM

SAMARIA

SHECHEM

PUZZLE 11: LEVITE CITIES

```
B A D D A N A T H O T H M D O L O I C B C
M F T G V B X H S E D E K Y Q R K N J J T
E A C A H E K E T L E X O B R G W C R P Z
O I H I L V P Q X E P G A E E O O R S V B
D X L A L E M K S C W E Y E S P R L H T N
X G O N N Z M I H C A Z T S C L H N I A R
D Z S A R A R E S N T Z I H T I I L L Z E
A W J T E N I E T K T L D T I B Q O N Z W
H L R R F U O M X H Y F M E J N G G A Y E
T C T A H H S M D W M M M R F A T J H F C
D K M K P U M R M Q S N P A K H O G A Q W
T N A P P C N A S I O H T H K J A X L I G
E T E A R A L L L B R C E G H N V C A O U
R N N B Q M W A H B D K O C B Q I Q L R S
A Z K J O D K S K T I D R L H E M U W V Y
E L O N T G E W T C A E H M B E O C U D F
P D J A F H D V D O V B R A M B M C M P C
F F P A N Y S R Q D R F O R Z M Z H Z S R
F B M A S H A L J A T T I R V H P R L W V
M B W D P U A N O R B E H X Z G A A K N J
W I T L C U D S N Z H U W X F G E J F S I
```

ALEMETH	JOKNEAM
ALMON	KARTAN
ANATHOTH	KEDESH
BEESHTERAH	LIBNAH
ELTEKEH	MAHANAIM
GOLAN	MASHAL
HEBRON	NAHALAL
HESHBON	RIMMON
JAHZAH	SHECHEM
JATTIR	TABOR

PUZZLE 12: PAUL'S JOURNEYS

```
X X Z A L A V S Q K X O J N D G S E N M F
W Y H Y R K U R X F N X K U W A H R A Q S
P F C T G P C R U T E J B E R A U Y N E T
M I S T I U S R A I S A V N R I B T T J L
A Y O S N K M J R U S V D E X N S Z I O T
L Q K K E P Y V R I O W B L H O C G O M D
V Z Z D T B R R P C L F B Y G L Y M C A J
L C P U Q V N B O S O W U T A O S Z H M X
M B O T T J A G A L C K L I L P F H O E E
G P Y Z A Y R V H N Z Z D M A P X T N S N
A G A U D W B C S M O V X A T A W K I V B
C D Y S I L O P A E N K J I I T Y D S X W
H E A R H Z Y S L P D F M R A W M A E C E
P A T A R A E D L H V O C Y P R U S F X X
G I S Q V Z F T D I T Y H S N I H K B I B
E Q S Y Y E H J M P R P Z R D I T Q S X Y
A U G Z K R B X T R O A S G U A M G T D U
W E V C A G F Q Z K N S M H R F G P X G Y
A T J C G Y S A L A M I S S K P U E N V B
G G E Q S V M I P U D W U D R P W Y D U O
E U S F U Y F Y K Y U S F W S P C V S R V
```

ANTIOCH
APPOLONIA
ASIA
COLOSSE
CYPRUS
GALATIA
LYCIA
LYSTRA
MITYLENE
NEAPOLIS

PATARA
RHODES
SALAMIS
SMYRNA
SYRIA
TARSUS
THRACE
TROAS
TYRE

PUZZLE 13: VILLAINS

```
I R M O C C P N X P C E P J P E H E R O D
T B Q A B A O N U U T O B I A H Y D Z V I
M W I F D N I G V X U I K W M F C D H F S
D N W M M M D A L E Y J K A S A M Y L E I
N E A A T X K W P Q V Q W G A V K H N G P
H H B J A H N M B H T Z C R C U M N P U L
T M B V M Z L W M O A U J Q P R A L T T E
A Y P O Y T W Z Q M R S H W R C L E J I H
I D L D R B U U Z U Q R O J H N I D N B P
L L A Z Q I M W S N Q F A E C Q P P L Z O
O T O E N O I N F A P H R E X T B J L E H
G M A U X E I U A T C I A S Y Y H P H D T
O A R L F A Q K B A B N H P P R D T E E I
J Q A V L Q O P E S E I P Q Q Z B A K K H
D L A L J A J U S L M A Q R N S K B A I A
Q Y I V W A B B G E A N G M L D A T H A N
U V D C U E T N L M I M Q I Z P R G S H T
Z M M G L N Z K A M C D A G M I S Z B T T
K X R B D Z F D R S F N U X Q J J H A F R
V O I V S Y H O M H D Y S A D U J I R R D
L I K U J P D F L I G U F B N F G G G U C
```

AHITHOPHEL

AMALEK

AMNON

CAIAPHAS

CAIN

DATHAN

ELYMAS

GOLIATH

HEROD

JUDAS

NIMROD

OMRI

PHARAOH

RABSHAKEH

SANBALLAT

SATAN

SENNACHERIB

SHIMEL

TOBIAH

VILLAINS

ZEDEKIAH

PUZZLE 14: SPIRIT OR FLESH?

```
L K K K C W M B T N L D U B K T S H A M E
I S A O O N B R E G N A U O H Y J V A Y A
X R T Y K P Z U G S Q J O K G H T U E M K
I J G I O M K O P L R U S M X X D I R P M
V U B A E Q C W O H G S K Q R R H D N D J
I T G R S C U V H I E U I E I F J A U A U
K C K J W Z E Y G N O S J G T G S X H S V
V W E L I U G D R E Z O S A Y Y F M C M R
V W H W I H M E N X I T F R H C K J W I V
V L J X R T T V T C Q Y A U U A A Q S Q C
O F W F I T D A I P M D Z O F R I Y J L O
Y E I N I Q N N R I P E A C E F U L K H T
C P D B B Y G J S W L B G I G I D X T P Q
V J P E I O N W N Z I P I H S R O W B Z F
P G I A M Z E P O K N M V V I D L V K X D
M V M R H L R B I T A G N I R E F F U S F
G P G W N H I W T G D J I B Q T P U E E W
C S R A U O S S O R V G K P F R E O W T H
D U P I V Q E Z M I N W R P M U L R H A K
Z W R V D H D W E E L Z L Y U S O D R H M
N T J L A E G I I F N Q X R B T M I E T Y
```

ANGER

BITTERNESS

COURAGE

DECEIT

DESIRE

EMOTIONS

GRIEF

GUILE

HAPPY

HATE

HOPE

LOVE

PEACEFUL

PRIDE

REJOICING

SHAME

SUFFERING

TRUST

VANITY

WORSHIP

WRATH

PUZZLE 15: ESTHER

```
B A U W F H V M S D F L B N X M Q W O M U
P Y A S W D S T T A P N P Z C A W M V C L
Q X U C Z S J B N T O S U R E U S A H A Y
H E Z T F I N S A S E C I P S H C H I K C
U K F E S E S D V P H A F D A I G J J X Y
J Q N U H Z Q H R X U M G D U I Z X Z T X
H L E Q A H W C E H F M A E O N R Y U K Z
O R L N A Y T Z S W A S A C T E K A T R I
R Q R A S C R E U X S G E A H D E F P A D
B Q S B H R W C H A T Q B T W B B R E X A
A K W Z G Z K Y H M G S S E W H I D Q K H
Y M M M A W G R W K J E Y L C N T D D O G
Y C G G Z D Y T R H F N T A C A Y E T I Q
J M H N Q F I N I G R I V E Z C L S R N Q
T N C T I N A X Y A T B S Z B R K A G T F
S H W N R N I V D G B U G W K O S E P M Z
N A V O D J R O O T A C B I H W V L A E H
Y M C D K D P O K R O N J G F N S P K N X
B N A S B T G A M L O O U T S T W C V T R
X T Q H E E Y M K S Z C H O A W S G L S H
P N M D Y T A Y E F S X X P J K D U D J Q
```

ADOPTED	MORNING
AHASUERUS	OINTMENTS
BANQUET	PALACE
BEAUTY	PLEASED
CONCUBINES	PRINCES
CROWN	SERVANTS
ESTHER	SHAASHGAZ
FAVOR	SPICES
GIFTS	VIRGIN
HADASSAH	

PUZZLE 16: HEROES

```
W G G V N A P K R E G L C T H T Z Z I O T
P H N M N D B D A V I D U Z X R L P Z S N
T F L X A L B Q U G T S G T H U O P A A L
H G T N Z Y O Z E I J Q C D L A G Z Y M O
N A I B S Q C F G D C O Q R L W C R W S J
J E I B G L A M J E A T C V B T O I C O O
L P T M B J J J X O G A I G D H L L M N E
K Y X W E J N F A N Z R U W R E G E T C L
V O B T P R A S Z E P U N D B E H V Z C A
E M B I R U E C R H G U Z A K H N Q A V B
O E Z A D D F J I N X W Q V O J U J L S V
F P J Q D I N W B S M I R Y S O K K P P T
G M T J Y I P F L H A G D G A R Z E O E R
W F R T H L A Y E J S I H Y U G L E B H V
W Z Y B F A Z H U O N K A E L S F R M I N
G Q H Z Q L R L M F X T V H U X E U U T O
J U Y C H E B A A L H X N M X E F N Y D A
U J F E H N R B S C V E T T Y C T W O Q H
T I K T S I V W U L F A Q E I L T V F C P
K O S R E Q R P R J M Y Y S B A H A R Q H
H E N J H L K B D H E R O E S K O C O S K
```

ABEL	JACOB
AMOS	JEREMIAH
DANIEL	JOEL
DAVID	MICAH
ENOCH	NOAH
ESTHER	OBADIAH
EZRA	RAHAB
GIDEON	SAMSON
HEROES	SAMUEL
ISAIAH	SARAH

PUZZLE 17: WATERWAYS

```
V N N M D F K G R X S T S I V Q W O F F C
D D V L O U F U W A T E R S L B M N H A Q
K W Z Y B R D A M A S C U S L C B E S O R
H O A Y M Y E L W X D H O U H E Z Z X L H
A C C Q Z Z J M F D Z U K E E V I M J Z L
L Q N L A A W N G T W Q R I H T N I V A P
U X C D B B B A D H A I M R B I A P T F F
S F R B N T A N C W T T E U M G K A Z T U
B E O F O I B F S H Z W O L A R N M N V S
A K S U S L Q Z Y J A F H D D I Z R K A L
C G C D B I T T E R U N F Z N S D C E P I
L Q I H R G N X M T I P B X J M J G W G G
X V Y Y N Y S K F R Q Y L H L R E F R Z J
U E M A E G C E R N X J D X R A K Z L E O
L B F G R Y I F E Q A F C Y N U I M O R R
L M I M Z M C I N O N R A V O O T N H E D
P W A P E U U J W C A S P A I N Q B R D A
M L T E J M F K D Y U W I G O X V W Y U N
D Y K P S Z R O B Q J F U S Y K H E K O H
E B K L Y B B Y G U E L O Q N L U V J S B
Z H Z C P E K J I R O H I H S D U R A B S
```

ADHAIM	JABBOK
ADREA	JORDAN
AEGEAN	LATANI
AQABA	MEROM
ARNON	SHIHOR
BESOR	TIGRIS
BITTER	URNIA
CASPAIN	WATERS
CHERITH	YARMUK
DAMASCUS	ZERED
HALUS	

PUZZLE 18: ASSASSINS

```
S G Q Y B A F U T I T H L Q I W E X N G H
W S S J U H Q J L D R V M X E A V K Q F R
A N E K A N O I E D J C R A I S H M A E L
A N G Z Q B M M L X M L U W I W T M A O L
F M A F F I A O T T K H U X Q L L H E J C
U E A N H S H L P D E D I O Q A W J H D L
L D Z S R V A A S J U S Y H P Z C N S C F
Q V D R A E D S M D F R N B H Q C V O P L
B I D U H E O B U A B Q I I Q L O Q H A W
B F A X Q N N A J K N B Q Q S L W A Q W N
Z V Y R A B I M E L E C H T W S S G F E S
R Y J E Q I J X A Q A J N A H T A U N Z K
Q R V D K N A V N H M E N L R V V S H M B
K I G N W P H Q S J O Z A L I A D T S V X
N E C A U Y G A M E D L I A X B R E I A O
B K M X A C A U N A O J C B S N A O F H S
X S D E G B A U C A R Q E N N N L G A W F
I F M L T F I N M A T E P A O E D K I T W
O C Y A C C G Z Q U I V H S E R E T K B G
N Z T B K K G P P R X X P X L P V V Q B V
F A H M P R B U E P E T Z X Z A U F Q W M
```

ABIMELECH	HAZEL
ABSALOM	HOSHEA
ADONIJAH	ISHMAEL
ALEXANDER	JEHU
AMASA	JOZALIAD
ASSASSINS	PEKAH
BAASHA	SANBALLAT
DEMAS	SHIMI
EHUD	TERESH
HAMAN	ZIBA

PUZZLE 19: JESUS AT THE TEMPLE

```
W C Q U E S T I O N S P S C G N I R A E H
J E R U S A L E M G F N H W A H E D W X Y
H R S K N F V Q J W M Q Q S T C R E Q L E
U R E T I V N O F C V D T P E I J R I O Y
C Q K H A P W A K Z Z O P G M J T Y X O F
H G B U T T N I G N N X V V P Z R Z C G H
R B R A V A U S S I S I E Q L H C X B N I
I E I V D U F R S I F R S S E T Y R B I K
S R O T C O D H E G L Y B Y A M A Z E D K
T J A M U X E R D F M Z J A K D T Q D N M
A N R Z Q D B I A K O H F D A E Z A K A Y
U N H P E S O J N Q D P T E H I N S R T G
G V O X P U J F Y Z S T U E S R L O G S O
V T W E L V E O I A I E Y R R R J V J R X
Q Y P S L E K V N Q W F K H E A B W X E C
A L K E U I E T B E W M J T W T Z W O D V
I S U B J E C T E T N C T Y S R X A F N H
L D K S G I F B Q Y Y D X L N S Q I N U S
I M K M E D N B H R G B E W A L K C J O K
I B W W G X U K Y S G U T I H E U I T T N
P Q Y G U X F G R W Z S N K R J W L L M H
```

AMAZED	QUESTIONS
ANSWERS	STATURE
ASTONISHED	SUBJECT
CHRIST	TARRIED
DOCTORS	TEMPLE
FATHER	THREE DAYS
HEARING	TWELVE
JERUSALEM	UNDERSTANDING
JOSEPH	WISDOM
NAZARETH	

PUZZLE 20: ROCKY ROAD

```
O  T  J  U  M  A  F  P  D  A  Q  B  S  Y  P  Z  Q  U  L  K  G
N  Z  C  F  M  Q  G  O  F  F  C  N  N  V  Z  E  G  Y  C  L  Y
W  Z  R  I  S  F  O  D  P  T  I  D  Z  Q  I  V  H  A  J  O  S
J  P  Z  I  H  O  G  B  W  A  M  M  A  H  O  V  X  C  A  E  C
A  A  N  B  O  M  N  W  T  L  B  L  K  S  N  K  C  N  I  S  O
R  A  N  Y  R  N  H  N  F  J  G  T  L  U  L  G  N  R  C  I  H
I  Q  M  N  E  I  U  N  O  M  R  E  H  S  I  J  B  N  E  R  F
X  C  O  L  B  O  H  N  H  K  M  U  X  W  K  U  G  S  Y  V  W
L  T  R  G  M  T  L  J  U  R  X  A  I  N  O  L  T  O  P  N  K
B  N  I  A  I  R  A  M  A  S  Y  R  G  Z  L  N  N  I  W  L  X
N  A  A  V  K  P  C  C  G  R  C  C  F  U  H  Z  S  M  R  O  M
C  E  H  E  D  U  M  J  Z  F  V  I  O  Z  F  G  K  O  F  S  H
B  L  C  I  X  S  C  G  X  X  V  C  G  K  A  Y  B  Q  H  N  B
G  I  U  H  C  P  S  S  S  K  A  L  A  H  T  A  R  A  C  U  W
A  L  D  K  Q  X  M  Z  S  R  A  M  H  L  T  S  D  A  Q  S  V
R  A  D  B  S  P  R  A  K  E  R  R  P  W  S  U  F  V  O  H  I
E  G  E  J  B  A  L  X  Q  H  G  L  B  M  J  C  B  A  W  Z  K
B  Q  W  Y  T  W  K  O  P  Y  M  A  L  K  Q  E  E  E  H  A  P
L  K  R  M  T  Y  E  B  U  A  V  H  X  K  C  G  D  X  V  G  M
W  I  G  S  Q  X  V  E  S  V  Y  A  Y  D  R  Z  W  O  C  U  T
Q  J  F  C  S  V  K  N  G  T  T  T  N  E  K  O  A  B  K  Y  S
```

AMMAH	MIZAR
CARMEL	MORIAH
GAASH	MOUNTAINS
GALILEAN	NEBO
GAREB	PISGAH
HALAK	SAMARIA
HERMON	SEIR
HOREB	SINAI
JUDAH	TABOR
MARS	ZION

WORD SEARCH SOLUTIONS

PUZZLE 1: Lessons

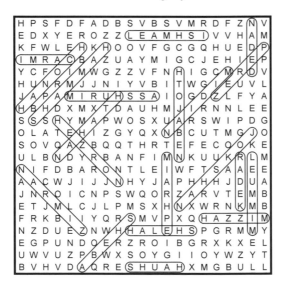

PUZZLE 2: Abraham's Progeny

PUZZLE 3: Prisoners and Captives

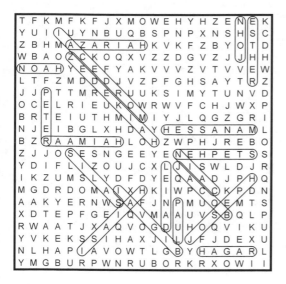

PUZZLE 4: Daniel

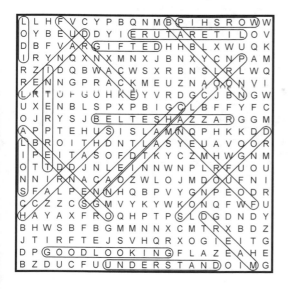

PUZZLE 5: The Tabernacle

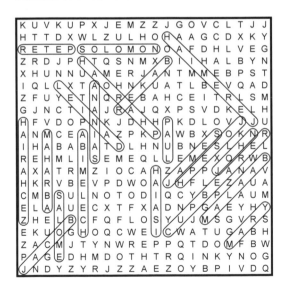

```
Z M R P T J J E S D F C I L Q B V B B O F
Y R A U T C N A S E H S L N V Z F Z G Q L
L K J M B J P Q M R I Y H S T I B U C I Z
R S Q J B G P Q Q A W L H O A S C G S N Z
G F T A J D D O G T C J O W W R N Q I C N
G D R K X L Z Q O Z K D H Q B S Q U E E
N N U B R Y U D V N I A L A F S R H F N L
L A O E M Q N E O E E U F I J O T E F S C
I T C L U F N O J M Z U Z C L C Y I A E A
X S R L U A Q S U E R H T A K G W L P D N
U P E O N B A J G N F J L C R D B O O R R
Z M N T T X K Q I I R W Z A J H K V S H E
Q A N D L S U S D K Z X F V X M T U V V B
W L U S J C H Z D E T C E R E W N S I U A
Z H B S R I V J L C N G U R O F U H Y A T
Q S V S N O N Z P N X M C E R D S V H F I
S E G G G L L Q B X Y K P E V S F D F J
X I S L A N X O G Y S N K B V X L G W A Y
N F H Z Y L M R Q E U R S W A R I V E Q E
D M M N N X L D A Z H Y G J U N Y F L Q Y
Q J F G F G J T S I K M N V S M R O U E D
```

PUZZLE 6: Dreamers

```
K U V K U P X J E M Z Z J G O V C L T J J
H T T D X W L Z U L H O H A A G C D X K Y
R E T E P S O L O M O N O A F D H L V E G
Z R D J P H T Q S N M X B I I H A L B Y N
X H U N N U A M E R J A N T M M E B P S T
I Q L L X T A O H N K U A T L B E V Q A D
Z F U Y E T N Q R E B A H C E I T R L S M
G J N C T I A J R A J Q X P S V D K E L H
H F V D O P N K J D H H P K D L O V J J U
A N M C E A I A Z P K P A W B X S O K N R
I H A B A B A T D L H N U B N E S L H E L
R E H M L I S E M E Q L U E M E X O R W B
A X A T R M Z I O C A H Z A P P J A N A V
H K R V B E V P D W O A J H F L E Z A U A
C M B S U L N O T O D I Q C Y B P L A U M
E L A A U E C X T F X A D N P G A E Y H Y
Z H E L B C F Q F L O S Y U J M S G V R S
E K U O G H O Q C W E U C W A T U G A B H
Z A C M J T Y N W R E P P Q T D O M F B W
P A G E D H M D O T H T R Q I N K Y N O G
U N D Y Z Y R J Z Z A E Z O Y B P I V D Q
```

PUZZLE 7: Kin to King Saul

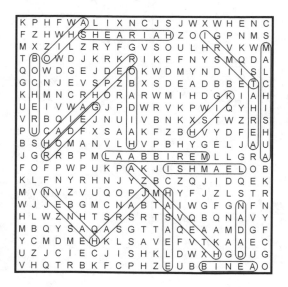

PUZZLE 8: Judah's Offspring

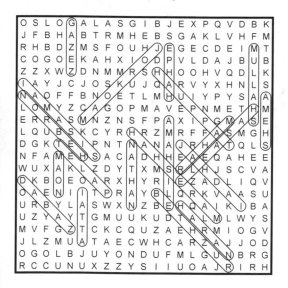

```
Y V S J T T F L M T T W Q D Q P S C I E Y
C R W N A M J C Y W H W P C A E A H B M S
Z W P F B N T M E L W E M V P R G V Q B P
N V F A A O N Q E E B S L U N E A L V A C
V G L Q A J E C B H K E D E Z I H C L E M
D A W A F E N P M P P F R H U S H A M N S
K H G V P H A R O A H X A H S R I B Y K N
I C V N H B L Q B R H K X K S M A X H U M
S E V T B A I K T M J E U B D R X M I B O
J L S B T A V Q Y A W H C F I W M H A C C
K E C W S L B L D A J F A O Z L H B A H W
M M P B H H S P A C A E C X L F O C E U A
I I D U N A T W D Z P H J N U J P D A X L
T B T P Z N B I A S H U A V V C O P R M E
E A L D B A N I H S I U B P M R D X H E B
G Q I N D N N T K W A I I I L B K N Z K U
S T D S J F O F D D J M N A M F B V K E O
F E X L F U T V D B X G O H A Q G Q T R N
I T Y A A U E R T U Q M X Q R V V I J Y S
U M O M M N P R P S E M Z R I G F B K Z T
X H O H A M R M G R E A G G Q P X Q A V V
```

PUZZLE 10: Altars

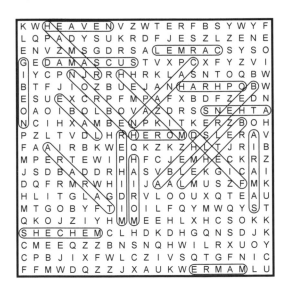

```
K W H E A V E N V Z W T E R F B S Y W Y F
L Q P A D Y S U K R D F J E S Z L Z E N E
E N V Z M S G D R S A L E M R A C S Y S O
G E D A M A S C U S T V X P C X F Y Z V I
I Y C P N J R R H H R K L A S N T O Q B W
B T F J I O Z B U E J A N H A R H P O B W
E S U E X C R P F M P A F X B D F Z E D N
O A O I B O L B O V A Z D R S S N E H T A
N C I H X A M B E N P K I T K E R Z B O H
P Z L T V D L H R H E R O M D S L E R A V
F A A I R B K W E Q K Z K Z H L J R I I B
M P E R T E W I P H F C J E M H E C K R Z
J S D B A D D R H A S V B L E K G I C A I
D Q F R M R W H I I J A A L M U S Z F M K
H L I T G L A G D R V L O O U X Q T E A U
M T G O B Y F T I O I L F Q Y M W Q Y S T
Q K O J Z I Y H M M E E H L X H C S O K K
S H E C H E M C L H D K D H G Q N S D J K
C M E E Q Z Z B N S N Q H W I L R X U O Y
C P B J I X F W L C Z I V S Q T G F N I C
F F M W D Q Z Z J X A U K W E R M A M L U
```

PUZZLE 11: Levite Cities

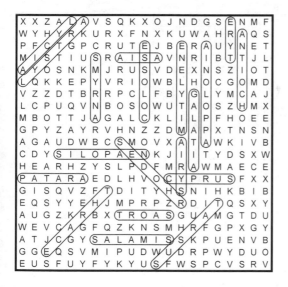

```
B A D D A N A T H O T H M D O L O I C B C
M F T G V B X H S E D E K Y Q R K N J J T
E A C A H E K E T L E X O B R G W C R P Z
O I H I L V P Q X E P G A E E O O R S V B
D X L A E M K S C W E Y E S P R L H T N
X G O N N Z M I H C A Z T S C L H N I A R
D Z S A R A R E S N T Z I H T I I L L Z E
A W J T E N I E T K T L D T I B O O N Z W
H L R R F U O M X H Y F M E J N G G A Y E
T C T A H H S M D W M M M R F A T J H F C
D K M K P U M R M Q S N P A K H O G A Q W
T N A P P C N A S I O H T H K J A X L I G
E T E A R A L L L B R C E G H N V C A O U
R N N B O M W A H B D K O C B Q I Q R S
A Z K J O D K S K T I D R L H E M U W V Y
E L O N T G E W T C A E H M B E O C U D F
P D U J A F H D V D O V B R A M B M C M P C
F F P A N Y S R Q D R F O R Z M Z H Z S R
F B M A S H A L J A T T I R V H P R L W V
M B W D P U A N O R B E H X Z G A A K N J
W I T L C U D S N Z H U W X F G E J F S I
```

PUZZLE 12: Paul's Journeys

```
X X Z A D A V S Q K X O J N D G S E N M F
W Y H Y R K U R X F N X K U W A H R A Q S
P F C T G P C R U T E J B E R A U Y N E T
M I S T I U S R A I S A V N R I B T T J L
A Y O S N K M J R U S V D E X N S Z I O T
L Q K K E P Y V R I O W B L H O C G O M D
V Z Z D T B R R P C L F B Y G L Y M C A J
L C P U Q V N B O S O W U T A O S Z H M X
M B O T T J A G A L C K L I L P F H O E E
G P Y Z A Y R V H N Z Z D M A P X T N S N
A G A U D W B C S M O V X A T A W K I V B
C D Y S I L O P A E N K J I I T Y D S X W
H E A R H Z Y S L P D F M R A W M A E C E
P A T A R A E D L H V O C Y P R U S F X X
G I S Q V Z F T D I T Y H S N I H K B I B
E Q S Y Y E H J M P R P Z R D I T Q S X Y
A U G Z K R B X T R O A S G U A M G T D U
W E V C A G F Q Z K N S M H R F G P X G Y
A T J C G Y S A L A M I S S K P U E N V B
G G E Q S V M I P U D W U D R P W Y D U O
E U S F U Y F Y K Y U S F W S P C V S R V
```

PUZZLE 13: Villains

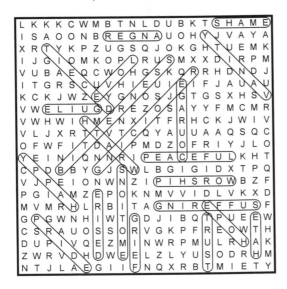

```
I R M O C C P N X P C E P J P E H E R O D
T B Q A B A N U U T O B I A H Y D Z V I
M W I F D N I G V X U I K W M F C D H F S
D N W M M M D A L E Y J K A S A M Y L E I
N E A A T X K W P Q V Q W G A V K H N G P
H H B J A H N M B H T Z C R C U M N P U L
T M B V M Z L W M O A U J Q P R A L T T E
A Y P O Y T W Z Q M R S H W R C L E J I H
I D L D R B U U Z U Q R O J H N I D N B P
L L A Z Q I M W S N Q F A E C Q P P L Z O
O T Q E N O I N F A P H R E X T B J L E H
G M A U X E I U A T C I A S Y Y H P H D T
O A R L F A Q K B A B N H P P R D T E E I
J Q A V L Q O P E S E I P Q Q Z B A K K H
D L A L J A J U S L M A Q R N S K B A I A
Q Y I V W A B B G E A N G M L D A T H A N
U V D C U E T N L M I M Q I Z P R G S H T
Z M M G L N Z K A M C D A G M I S Z B T T
K X R B D Z F D R S F N U X Q J J H A F R
V O I V S Y H O M H D Y S A D U J I R R D
L I K U J P O F L I G U F B N F G G G U C
```

PUZZLE 14: Spirit or Flesh?

```
L K K K C W M B T N L D U B K T S H A M E
I S A O O N B R E G N A U O H Y J V A Y A
X R T Y K P Z U G S Q J O K G H T U E M K
I J G I O M K O P L R U S M X X D R P M
V U B A E Q C W O H G S K Q R H D N D J
I T G R S C U V H I E U I E I F J A U A U
K C K J W Z E Y G N O S J G T G S X H S V
V W E L I U G D R E Z O S A Y Y F M C M R
V W H W I H M E N X I T F R H C K J W I V
V L J X R T T V T C Q Y A U U A A Q S Q C
O F W F I T D A I P M D Z O F R I Y J L O
Y E I N I Q N N R I P E A C E F U L K H T
C P D B B Y G J S W L B G I G I D X T P Q
V J P E I O N W N Z I P I H S R O W B Z F
P G I A M Z E P O K N M V V I D L V K X D
M V M R H L R B I T A G N I R E F F U S F
G P G W N H I W T G D J I B Q T P U E E W
C S R A U O S S O R V G K P F R E O W T H
D U P I V Q E Z M I N W R P M U L R H A K
Z W R V D H U W E E L Z L Y U S O D R H M
N T J L A E G I I F N Q X R B T M I E T Y
```

PUZZLE 15: Esther

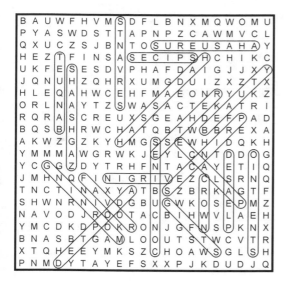

PUZZLE 16: Heroes

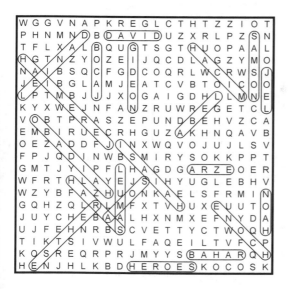

PUZZLE 17: Waterways

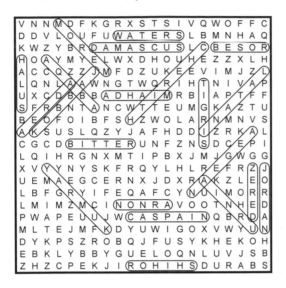

PUZZLE 18: Assassins

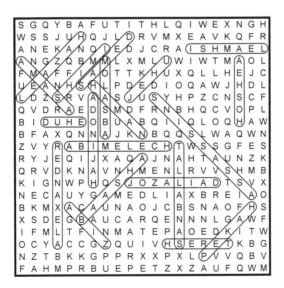

PUZZLE 19: Jesus at the Temple

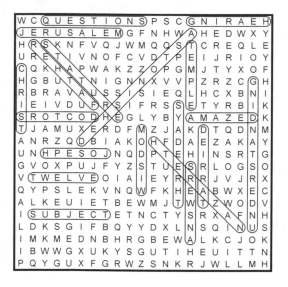

PUZZLE 20: Rocky Road

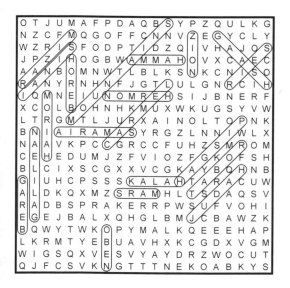

SCORE SHEET

PUZZLES (1 POINT PER PUZZLE)	POINTS
Cryptograms (60)	
Crossword Puzzles (5)	
Sudoku (50)	
Word Search (20)	
Total	

Add the total scores from all four units. Based on your total score, receive your crown!

Total score = 0–50: You are hereby crowned "Sunday-school dropout"—Superior level.

Total score = 51–80: You are hereby crowned "Sunday-school graduate"—Superior level.

Total score = 81–94: You are hereby crowned "Biblically knowledgeable"—Superior level.

Total score = 95–104: You are hereby crowned "Bible trivia master"—Superior level.

Total score = 105–114: You are hereby crowned "Bible scholar of the highest order"—Superior level.

Total score = 115–135: You are hereby crowned "Honorary doctor of theology"—Superior level.

The book of Proverbs, along with the book of Job, Ecclesiastes and Song of Solomon, is considered to be wisdom literature. Proverbs, in particular, has five very specific teachings vital to expanding our brainpower.

Proverbs 1:2 To know wisdom and instruction; to perceive the words of understanding;

Proverbs 1:3 To receive the instruction of wisdom, justice, and judgment, and equity;

Proverbs 1:4 To give subtlety to the simple, to the young man knowledge and discretion;

Proverbs 1:5 A wise man will hear and increase in learning, And a man of understanding will acquire wise counsel

Proverbs 1:6 To understand a proverb, and the interpretation; the words of the wise, and their dark sayings.

Proverbs 1:7, however, is the most vital Scripture for our learning foundation.

"The fear of the Lord is the beginning of wisdom, But fools despise wisdom and instruction."

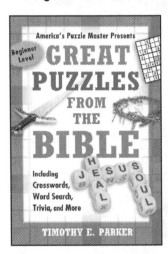
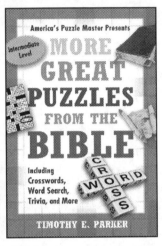
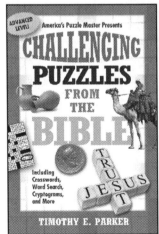

Printed in the United States
By Bookmasters